T0339913

Reframing Energy Access

This book investigates energy access through the lens of everyday energy practices in the Gambian community of Kartong.

Reframing Energy Access: Insights from The Gambia explores past, current and potential future modes of energy production and consumption to examine concepts such as energy leapfrogging and energy sufficiency. It argues that developments must be rooted in situated understanding of energy consumption to ensure sustainable and equitable access to modern energy services. Schiffer provides a uniquely long-term and holistic perspective into changing energy practices on the ground and the economic, political, environmental, technical and cultural factors that shape it.

Translating insights of energy in The Gambian context into broader themes and recommendations, this book will be of great interest to policy makers, researchers and practitioners who work in the fields of energy access, energy policy, renewable energy transitions, as well as African and sustainable development in general.

Anne Schiffer is Senior Lecturer in the Leeds School of Arts, Leeds Beckett University, UK.

Routledge Focus on Environment and Sustainability

Design for Sustainability
A Multi-level Framework from Products to Socio-technical Systems
Fabrizio Ceschin and İdil Gaziulusoy

Sustainability, Conservation and Creativity
Ethnographic Learning from Small-scale Practices
Pamela J. Stewart and Andrew J. Strathern

Jainism and Environmental Politics
Aidan Rankin

Australian Climate Policy and Diplomacy
Government-Industry Discourses
Ben L. Parr

Climate and Energy Politics in Poland
Debating Carbon Dioxide and Shale Gas
Aleksandra Lis

Sustainable Community Movement Organizations
Solidarity Economies and Rhizomatic Practices
Edited by Francesca Forno and Richard R. Weiner

Reframing Energy Access
Insights from The Gambia
Anne Schiffer

For more information about this series, please visit: www.routledge.com/ Routledge-Focus-on-Environment-and-Sustainability/book-series/RFES

Reframing Energy Access

Insights from The Gambia

Anne Schiffer

Routledge
Taylor & Francis Group

LONDON AND NEW YORK

earthscan
from Routledge

First published 2020 by Routledge

2 Park Square, Milton Park, Abingdon, Oxon OX14 4RN
605 Third Avenue, New York, NY 10017

Routledge is an imprint of the Taylor & Francis Group, an informa business

First issued in paperback 2021

British Library Cataloguing-in-Publication Data
A catalogue record for this book is available from the British Library

Library of Congress Cataloging-in-Publication Data
Names: Schiffer, Anne, author.
Title: Reframing energy access : insights from the Gambia / Anne Schiffer.
Other titles: Routledge focus on environment and sustainability.
Description: New York : Routledge, 2020. | Series: Routledge focus on
   environment and sustainability | Includes bibliographical references and
   index.
Identifiers: LCCN 2019058564 (print) | LCCN 2019058565 (ebook) |
   ISBN 9781138311695 (hardback) | ISBN 9780429458699 (ebook)
Subjects: LCSH: Energy consumption—Gambia—Kartong. | Energy
   development—Social aspects—Gambia—Kartong. | Energy
   development—Government policy—Gambia. | Energy policy—
   Social aspects—Gambia. | Sustainable development.
Classification: LCC HD9502.G265 S35 2020 (print) | LCC HD9502.
   G265 (ebook) | DDC 333.7915096651—dc23
LC record available at https://lccn.loc.gov/2019058564
LC ebook record available at https://lccn.loc.gov/2019058565

ISBN: 978-1-138-31169-5 (hbk)
ISBN: 978-1-03-217276-7 (pbk)
DOI: 10.4324/9780429458699

Typeset in Times New Roman
by Apex CoVantage, LLC

For the people of Kartong. Fo wati do.

Contents

Maps

Figures

Acknowledgements

Over the past decade, there have been many people and organisations who have supported and contributed to the research which has led to this book. Thank you to Annabelle Harris and Hannah Ferguson at Routledge who prompted and supported me in developing the initial book proposal and Matthew Shobbrook for helping me see it through.

I gratefully acknowledge financial support I received through the BA/ Leverhulme Trust Small Grants scheme which led to renewed insight into local visions for Kartong energy futures in 2019. I would also like to acknowledge funding received through the H2020 SHAPE Energy Research Design Challenge which enabled me to collaborate on research investigating energy pasts with Dr Mary Greene.

I would like to thank my former PhD supervisors Professor Greg Keeffe and Professor John Barry at Queen's University Belfast for their support, advice and encouragement. I could not have asked for a better supervisory team. Thank you also to former academic staff at Leeds Beckett University including Rupert Bozeat and Elspeth Jones for bringing me to The Gambia in the first place as well as Louise Dixey who introduced me to feminist development literature. Thank you to Dr Alma Clavin, Professor Guy Julier, Wendy Mayfield and those who supported me especially in the early days. Thank you also to Melissa Rezaei and Peter Hamilton for their digital support and Dr Anna Watson for introducing me to 'asset mapping.'

My gratitude further extends to an array of people, collaborators and organisations who have shaped my understanding of policies and concepts associated with energy access and energy transitions. This includes former partners in the Community Power project (www.communitypower.eu) and the Scottish Community Energy Coalition, Lucy Cadena at Friends of the Earth International, Niclas Hallström at WhatNext Forum?, Brandon Wu at ActionAid USA, Dr Paul Munro at the University of New South Wales and the wider Friends of the Earth family. In The Gambia I would like thank Nani Juwara at the National Water and Electricity Company for discussing infrastructure and policy developments and Lamin Jarjou at UNESCO for making introductions to a range of high-level stakeholders working on broader energy issues facing The Gambia.

Several people have kindly reviewed or proofread versions of written materials. I would like to express my gratitude to Dr Mary Greene, Lamin Jarjou, John Thackara and especially my very patient husband Dr Andrew J.D. Matson.

Most importantly, I would like to acknowledge and thank the people of Kartong without whom this research would not have been possible and who have become friends, teachers and collaborators. I am especially grateful to my hosts Sankung Sambou and Maimuna Tourey, Bah-Musa Sambou and the extended Sambou family for enabling me to be part of local life. Thank you to those who enthusiastically helped organise, shape and facilitate workshops or support community mapping including Isatou Manneh, Momodou Mbye Jabang, Ismaila Jarjou, Foday Juwara, Badibu, Ismaila, Kanjura, Sankung and Sulayman Sambou.

A big thanks to all Kartonkas who have at some point contributed to the research by taking part in semi-structured interviews, workshops, countless informal conversations, invited me into their homes and businesses, answered my endless questions about factors that shape local energy pratices or simply positively engaged with me during my visits to Kartong. I would hereby also like to formally thank the Alkalo and members of the Village Development Committee.

Abaraka bake.

Abbreviations

CBF	Community Benefit Fund
CRELUZ	Cooperativa de Energia e Desenvolvimento Rural do Medio Uruguai Ltda
ECOWAS	Economic Community of West African States
EV	Electric Vehicle
FIT	Feed-In Tariff
FOEI	Friends of the Earth International
IEA	International Energy Agency
ICT	Information and Communication Technology
IRENA	International Renewable Energy Agency
LED	Light Emitting Diode
NAWEC	National Water and Electricity Company
NGO	Non-Governmental Organisation
PURA	Public Utilities Regulatory Authority
SDG	Sustainable Development Goals
TDA	Tourism Development Area
UNFCCC	United Nations Framework Convention on Climate Change
VDC	Village Development Committee

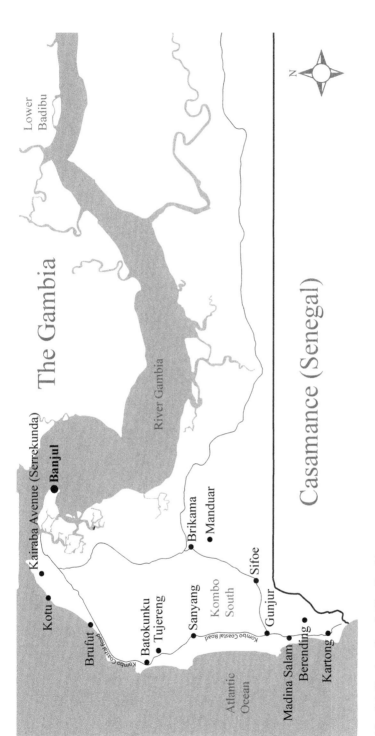

Map 0.1 Key locations in The Gambia

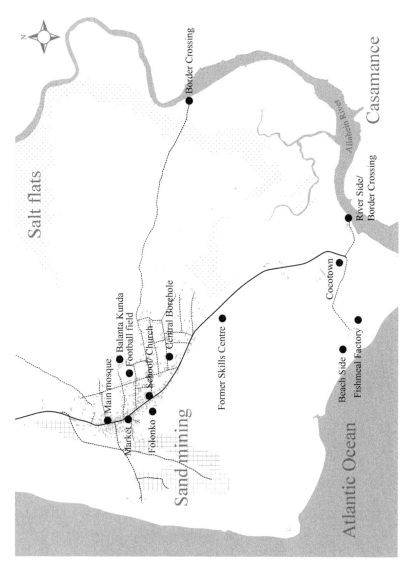

Map 0.2 Places in Kartong

1 Introduction

Why we need human insights into everyday energy practices

When first visiting The Gambia during brief excursions in 2008 and 2009, I was struck by the amount of obsolete equipment and infrastructure dotted around the smallest country in mainland Africa. I came across a large solar water-heating system installed at a cooking school that had fallen into disrepair and was covered in dust; the remnants of wind-powered water pumps along coastal towns; a car ferry with a broken motor that passengers had to pull across a narrow part of the River Gambia using a rope; an ultrasound scanner rendered useless because it was not possible to replace a defective part and a broken-down second-hand ambulance in an up-country hospital. I saw poorly maintained solar systems for production of electricity at household level; a room full of defunct computers in a community skills centre and different types of solar cookers that were either too expensive or were unsuitable for local cooking cultures and had therefore not been adapted.

A lot of the equipment and infrastructure mentioned above had been sponsored by well-meaning donors, small non-governmental organisations or received European Union funding at some stage in the past. That did not change the fact that what often remained were mere 'ornaments,' using the words of a Gambian doctor as he pointed at a broken computer in a small health clinic.

Originally trained as a product designer, I was concerned with improving the everyday and it seemed that here the intended 'users,' including their needs, capacities and aspirations, had been ill-considered in what appeared to be techno-centric approaches to local energy challenges. At that point in my career I had limited experience of working in a developing world context and it was therefore easy to criticise what I perceived as failed interventions.

However, in 2010, I became involved in a university volunteering project that aimed to teach people in the coastal community of Kartong[1] how to build small wind turbines. At the time there was no electricity grid in the community and a small turbine could potentially generate additional power to charge equipment such as mobile phones which relied on off-grid generating capacity. Over a three-week period we had passed on skills about how to construct and maintain the machines to a local group of people and left them with a small turbine that just needed to find a permanent home. As one of the volunteers commented a few days before our departure: "It feels really good to know that we are helping a community to develop and teaching them skills that will stay with most of them forever." Similarly, a local participant expressed high hopes: "About the experience they are giving to us. [We] have learnt a lot about wind turbines. We are going to build our own."

I returned to The Gambia during the rainy season several months later for the purpose of PhD-related field research. A core group of local people were keen to take the wind turbine project forward. However, apart from my time and limited technical expertise (I had previously participated in a short course on how to build small wind turbines at the Centre for Alternative Technology in Wales), I had little to offer. Eventually the turbine was installed on a short pole on top of the local skills centre, generating electricity to charge gadgets for a brief period. However, positioned in close proximity to the roof of the building, the turbine was exposed to turbulence that is likely to have contributed to repeated failure and eventually led to irreparable damage.

On reflection, there were many issues with the project. These related to available finance, volunteer capacity, lack of time and resources to carry out a feasibility study prior to the project or provide continued support, as well as conflicting agendas of different stakeholder groups involved. As volunteers we saw local people as recipients of our good will and therefore failed to work directly with them as partners in the shaping and delivery of the project. Instead we relied on foreign intermediaries who hosted us and our activities several kilometres outside of Kartong. This physical distance contributed to a lacking sense of local ownership of the project.

Furthermore, we had very limited and largely second-hand insight into local energy practices to inform the project, let alone understanding about how these were changing over time. The absence of what designers refer to as 'human insight' coupled with a lack of local ownership were key in the overall failure of delivering long-term positive impact (Brown, 2009). With the best intentions, I was complicit in creating yet another well-intended ornament: an object without a practical function.

These early observations and experiences are part of a much larger story of failed infrastructural and technological energy interventions in which we did "what every donor does in Africa," which is "learn by trial and error" (Harden, 1993, p. 103). While this book is not a 'how-to guide' on successfully implementing energy infrastructure projects, it supports the increasing recognition that energy is not merely a technological challenge but is in fact 'deeply social' and intertwined with the fundamentals of everyday life (Shove and Walker, 2014). Therefore, both practical infrastructure and policy interventions need to be rooted in the understanding of this.

Nonetheless, considerations for energy access such as rural electrification programmes continue to be dominated by techno-centric approaches and top-down decision making. Oblivious to the realities of everyday lives, this in turn contributes to the continuing failure to ensure equitable and sustainable energy access. The book is intended to help bridge the gap between the lived experience of energy scarcity and external decision-making processes concerned with the delivery of energy access. It does so by fostering a broader understanding of situated energy practices and the complex dynamics which shape it, including people's "needs, preferences and aspirations" (Steen, 2011). As such, the book aims to translate human insight of changing and situated energy practices in Kartong into considerations and recommendations for those who work in the context of energy access delivery and sustainable energy transitions.

The book is written for three main audiences. Firstly, it is intended to provide rich human insight for those who are academically or otherwise engaged in a growing body of research concerned with energy and the everyday. To this end several chapters, Appendix 1 and the following introductory sections include an overview of how primary research was negotiated, the methods used and the conceptual frame that underpins it. Secondly, the book is aimed at those who deliver physical interventions in developing world contexts, such as charitable organisations and contractors. While the analysis is largely focused on The Gambia, the information therein is intended to provide an additional level of understanding regarding the complex dynamics which shape the adaptations of infrastructure and policy in everyday life and the need to carefully consider how interventions play out at the grassroots. Finally, the book makes a number of recommendations for decision makers and practitioners engaged in energy access at local, national and international levels.

Gaining insight into energy practices

Following the aforementioned volunteering project, I conducted three months of field research in The Gambia towards the end of 2010. I found accommodation in a British national's holiday home located in the neighbouring village of Madina Salam. From there, I cycled to Kartong most days and engaged in activities such as mapping infrastructure by walking through the settlement area with a printout of a Google satellite image. The process helped me to build relationships with local people who were curious about my intentions and ultimately led to a family hosting me on subsequent visits. Staying in a Kartong compound – the extended family home consisting of several households – enabled me to immerse myself, observe and participate in local life and so gain human insight into local energy practices. In particular, 'embodied' experiences where I physically engaged in activities such as transplanting rice, cooking food or traveling on local transport provided a deeper sense of empathy (Coffey, 1999).

These immersions were supported by a number of ethnographic and human-centred design research methods including semi-structured interviews and mapping. The latter refers to both spatial maps and abstract visualisations of otherwise unseen information (Brook and Dunn, 2013). The book also draws on insights gathered during a number of co-design workshops that engaged different stakeholder groups and enabled discussions about present challenges as well as preferences and aspirations regarding the future of energy in Kartong.

Moreover, the research which has informed this book is strengthened by two temporal considerations. Firstly, I have been able to witness drastic changes in local energy cultures over a decade of visiting The Gambia. Secondly, I have tried hard to avoid what Chambers (2012, p. 38) refers to as 'season blindness,' which is a limited or skewed understanding of a place and people's practices based on experience of only one (and typically the dry) season. As such, I have carried out field research in Kartong during the dry season which also coincides with the tourist season; Harmattan which is a time of year when dusty winds blow across from the Sahara Desert; the rainy season and during Ramadan. As will become apparent, these different periods of time are associated with changing practices that have implications for the extent to which energy access is negotiated.

In parallel to carrying out research in The Gambia, I was employed as a community energy campaigner based in Scotland for a number of years. I worked as part of a European funded project called Community Power (communitypower.eu) which aimed to improve policy and legislation for community-owned renewable energy schemes across Europe. A particular frustration I developed was in regard to the silos in which policies are created. Here, electricity targets are commonly set in isolation from transport strategies or land-use plans, an issue that transcends both industrialised and developing world contexts. Yet in everyday life different dimensions of energy are all experienced as part of the same system. Decisions aimed at affecting one component can lead to unintended consequences elsewhere or missed opportunities to bring about broader positive change.

Fortunately, repeated immersions in Kartong have provided me with a more holistic understanding of how energy is experienced and practised at a local level. This includes shifts in the way people communicate, use lighting, and travel within and outside of the settlement, as well as changing practices surrounding food. There is criticism of electricity dominating energy access debates in relation to developmental and climate change objectives, whereas other forms of energy have not drawn as much attention (Bhattacharyya, 2012; Brown et al., 2018). While some of the analysis of this book emphasises electricity in the context of developmental trajectories in Kartong, it is rooted in this much broader understanding of energy in everyday life, thereby transcending the aforementioned silos.

In order to understand energy in a more holistic and integrated manner, the analysis draws on the urban metabolism framework, which is widely established to assess the level of sustainability in relation to resource flows, in, out and within the urban environment. Here, circular resource flows or metabolisms are seen as sustainable and resilient (Spiller and Agudelo, 2011; Agudelo-Vera, 2012).

These circular resource flows can be compared to the metabolic processes of nature: "in which every output discharged by an organism also becomes an input which renews and sustains the continuity of the whole" (Girardet, 2008, p. 123; 1999, p. 32). In contrast, linear metabolisms which rely on resources that are brought in from the rural or sometimes global 'hinterland' and produce waste – including emissions – as they are being consumed, are seen as unsustainable and subsequently more vulnerable (Klindworth et al., 2017; European Development Agency, 2015, p. 26). As such, the urban metabolism framework is closely aligned to wider debates that link circularity with sustainable development including the 'circular economy' and circular methods of manufacture (Schwarz et al., 2016; McDonough and Braungart, 2002; Girardet, 2017).

The urban metabolism can be understood as a "collection of complex sociotechnical and socioecological processes by which flows of materials, energy, people, and information shape the city, service the needs of its populace, and impact the surrounding hinterland" (Currie and Musango, 2017). While Kartong is strictly speaking not yet urban,[2] the transition to modern energy services such as electricity is also marked by increasingly urban characteristics at the local level. The adaptation of the urban or more specifically the 'energy metabolism,' however, also recognises that regional and global 'hinterlands' do not just feed the city (Kennedy et al., 2007), but that the city itself also impacts on or is seen as responsible for providing rural communities with services, goods and infrastructure such as electricity grids and roads.

Traditionally, urban metabolism studies have been informed by predominately quantitative data (Musango et al., 2017; Serrano-Tovar and Giampietro, 2013; Hall, 2011). This is the case even with studies that emphasise the social dimensions in urban metabolism literature (Davis, 2016). However, there is recognition that more qualitative understanding such as knowledge of local people's perceptions is required to help make sense of how social structures intersect with wider dynamics that shape metabolic processes (Pistoni and Bonin, 2017). Again, this is also reflected in changing debates on circular approaches which need to "include human values, social qualities and human experiences as much as biological and physical attributes" (Schwarz et al., 2016, p. 104).

In this book, the energy metabolism is therefore understood through the lens of situated practices which is defined here as the culmination of socio-cultural, socio-technical, socio-environmental, socio-economic and socio-political dimensions that shape energy access in everyday life (Schiffer et al., 2019). This includes temporal, spatial and socially differentiated ways in which energy practices are carried out.

Chapter overview

The book is divided into two reciprocal strands: Chapters 2, 4 and 6 describe changing energy practices of Kartong's past, present and future. As such, they present human insight gathered over the research period to analyse the dynamics that shape the evolution of Kartong's energy metabolisms, including people's practices over time. In correspondence, Chapters 3, 5 and 7 reflect on the forgone insights to provide a critical perspective on wider debates surrounding energy access and energy transition research.

> *Chapter 2 – Remembering energy pasts: situated practices and historic changes.* The chapter introduces Kartong by exploring historic changes in local energy practices from a time when resources were predominately found locally. It establishes key themes related to socio-cultural, -environmental, -economic, -technical and -political dimensions that have shaped changing energy practices in the past.
>
> *Chapter 3 – Delivering sustainable energy access: an exploration of leapfrogging in Kartong.* This chapter investigates the notion of 'leapfrogging' by reflecting on historic energy practices. It draws on a number of examples from around the world to tease out wider considerations for leapfrogging and delivering energy access that are both environmentally sound and socially just.
>
> *Chapter 4 – Current energy practices: everyday life in a local compound of Samou Kunda.* The chapter examines the more recent transition to modern energy services in Kartong through the lens of everyday life in the Sambou compound. While there are clear benefits associated with services such as access to grid electricity, seasonal, spatial and gender dimensions also result in energy inequality across the community and a wider process of increasing fossil fuel dependence.

Chapter 5 – Enough is enough: considering energy sufficiency. Somewhere between the extremes of energy scarcity and overconsumption of energy lies what can be described as energy sufficiency. This chapter considers the broader practical implications of delivering sufficient access to modern energy services in light of ongoing changes in local energy cultures.

Chapter 6 – Kartong energy futures: local attitudes and opportunities for positive change. Based on co-design workshops with different stakeholder groups, this chapter explores people's aspirations for the future of energy in Kartong. It also uses insight gained to explore opportunities and structures for renewable alternatives.

Chapter 7 – Reframing energy access: situated insights as a chance for more equitable and sustainable consumption. The concluding chapter demonstrates the value of human insight into situated practices by summaries of key findings. It also provides a list of recommendations and considerations for policy makers and practitioners working on energy access.

A note on the wider context

Since the beginning of the research that has led to this book, The Gambia has experienced a number of wider challenges and changes which have impacted on energy practices as well as local life more broadly. In 2014 the deadly Ebola virus resurfaced in parts of West Africa and though it never reached The Gambia it scared off tourists, reducing opportunities for income generation along Africa's 'smiling coast.' Furthermore, the country transitioned to a new government under President Adama Barrow at the beginning of 2017, following his majority win in the foregone presidential election. Barrow defeated Yayha Jammeh, who had ruled The Gambia since coming to power in a coup d'état in 1994.

During Jammeh's reign I personally never felt in danger as my research was not uncovering political controversies. However, The Gambia's secret police had a notorious reputation and their actions recently came to light through investigations by The Gambia's Truth, Reconciliation and Reparations Commission. Under Jammeh it was therefore best to avoid any discussions of a political nature to prevent negative repercussions, especially for those connected to oneself. I was aware of the seemingly erratic government actions that switched between deporting homosexual foreigners, executing prisoners by firing squad, leaving the Commonwealth and banning the use of plastic bags. Despite his efforts to keep the opposition quiet, there was a growing push-back against Jammeh which included an attempted coup d'état that erupted in Banjul while I was visiting the country in December 2014. Two years later Jammeh was defeated by Adama Barrow but refused to leave until he was forced out of office under threat from military action by members of the Economic Community of West African States (ECOWAS).

Now several years into the new republic currently led by Adama Barrow, the book provides a timely perspective of changing energy practices in The Gambia, ongoing challenges and opportunities for more sustainable and socially just energy futures. It offers a uniquely long-term perspective of the interface between energy access and the broader dynamics that shape it in the context of everyday life.

Notes

1 Kartong is sometimes spelled Kartung.
2 A globally applicable definition for urban does not exist. The 2007 edition of the United Nations Demographic Yearbook gives definitions that vary from "agglomerations of 10 000 or more inhabitants" in Senegal to ambiguous descriptions such as "places with urban characteristics" in Indonesia or much more specific definitions like the one provided for the Netherlands: "Urban: Municipalities with a population of 2 000 and more inhabitants. Semi-urban: Municipalities with a population of less than 2 000 but with not more than 20 per cent of their economically active male population engaged in agriculture, and specific residential municipalities of commuters" (UN DESA, 2009). Others (e.g. Pickett, 2013, p. 162) include suburbs as well as exurbs used to describe geographically separated areas beyond the suburbs of the city when defining urban. Common factors in determining if a settlement area can be classed as urban are population size, economic activity and the availability of services such as electricity or healthcare. In The Gambia, one definition of urban is "settlements of more than 5,000 inhabitants with a health centre and electricity" as opposed to rural which does not meet these criteria (UN, 2012). In another publication urban is simply defined as aggregations of 5,000 people or more as it is assumed that the primary source of income has shifted from agricultural activities to trade in settlements of this size (International Business Publications, 2011, p. 35). However, obtaining up-to-date population census data in The Gambia can be difficult as it may take several years for it to be published despite the fact that a census is carried out every ten years. In 1963 the director of that year's population census claimed "To be accurate, there is no town in [T]he Gambia except that of Bathurst" the capital which was renamed Banjul in 1973 (Oliver, 1965, p. 25).

References

Agudelo-Vera, Leduc, W.R.W.A., Mels, A.R. and Rijnaarts, H.H.M. (2012) Harvesting urban resources towards more resilient cities. *Resources, Conservation and Recycling*, 64, pp. 3–12. DOI: 10.1016/j.resconrec.2012.01.014

Bhattacharyya, S.C. (2012) Energy access programmes and sustainable development: A critical review analysis. *Energy for Sustainable Development*, 16 (3), pp. 260–271. https://doi.org/10.1016/j.esd.2012.05.002

Brook, R. and Dunn, N. (2013) *Urban maps: Instruments of narrative and interpretation in the city*. Farnham: Ashgate Publishing.

Brown, E., Campbell, B., Cloke, J., Seng To, L., Turner, B. and Wry, A. (2018) Low carbon energy and international development: From research impact to policy-making. *Contemporary Social Science*, 13 (1), pp. 112–127. https://doi.org/10.10 80/21582041.2017.1417627

Brown, T. (2009) *Change by design: How design thinking transforms organizations and inspires innovation*. New York: Harper Business.

Chambers, R. (2012) *Provocations for development*. Warwickshire: Practical Action.

Coffey, A. (1999) *The ethnographic self: Fieldwork and the representation of iden-tify*. London: Sage Publications.

Currie, P.K. and Musango, J.K. (2017) African urbanization: Assimilating urban metabolism into sustainability discourse and practice. *Journal of Industrial Ecol-ogy*, 21 (5), pp. 1262–1276. https://doi.org/10.1111/jiec.12517

Davis, M.J.M., Jácome Polit, D. and Lamour, M. (2016) Social Urban Metabolism Strategies (SUMS) for cities: Improving sustainability concept in developing countries. *Procedia Environmental Sciences*, 34, pp. 309–327. DOI: 10.1016/j. proenv.2016.04.028

European Development Agency (2015) *Urban sustainability issues: What is a resource efficient city?* Copenhagen: European Development Agency.

Girardet, H. (2017) *Regenerative cities: Making cities work for people and planet*. Sydney: Cooperative Research Centre for Low Carbon Living.

Girardet, H. (2008) *Cities people planet: Urban development and climate change*. 2nd ed. Chichester: John Wiley & Sons.

Girardet, H. (1999) *Creating sustainable cities: Schumacher briefing, no. 2*. Fox-hole: Green Books.

Hall, M.H.P. (2011) A preliminary assessment of socio-ecological metabolism for three neighbourhoods within a rust belt urban ecosystem. *Ecological Modelling*, 223 (1), pp. 20–31. https://doi.org/10.1016/j.ecolmodel.2011.08.018

Harden, B. (1993) *Africa: Dispatches from a fragile continent*. 3rd ed. London: Harper Collins Publishers.

International Business Publications (2011) *Gambia: Foreign policy and government guide*. Volume 1. Washington: International Business Publications.

Kennedy, C., Cuddihy, J. and Engel-Yan, J. (2007) The changing metabolism of cit-ies. *Journal of Industrial Ecology*, 2 (11), pp. 43–59. DOI: 10.1162/jie.2007.1107

Klindworth, K., Djurasovic, A., Knieling, J. and Säwert, K. (2017) From linear to circular: Challenges for changing urban metabolism?! An analysis of local energy transition activities in four European cities. In: Deppisch, S. ed. *Urban regions now and tomorrow*. Wiesbaden: Springer.

McDonough, W. and Braungart, M. (2002) *Cradle to cradle: Remaking the way we make things*. 1st ed. New York: North Point Press.

Musango, J.K., Currie, P. and Robinson, B. (2017) *Urban metabolism for resource efficient cities: From theory to implementation*. Paris: UN Environment.

Oliver, H.A. (1965) Report on the census of population of the Gambia: Bathurst, government printer. Quoted in: Denis, E., Moriconi-Ebrard, F. and Agence française de développement eds. (2009) *Africapolis: Urbanization trends 1950–2020: A geo-statistical approach, West Africa*. Paris: Agence Française de Développement.

Pickett, S.T.A. (2013) Ecology of the city: A perspective from science. In: McGrath, B. ed. *Urban design ecologies*. Chichester: Wiley.

Pistoni, R. and Bonin, S. (2017) Urban metabolism planning and designing approaches between quantitative analysis and urban landscape. *City, Territory and Architecture*, 4 (20), pp. 1–11. https://doi.org/10.1186/s40410-017-0076-y

Schiffer, A., Swan, A., Mendes, R.L.R. and Vasconcellos Sobrinho, M. (2019) Looking to peripheral river islands in Brazil to develop an urban island water metabolism perspective. *Waterlines*, 38 (2), pp. 135–146. https://doi.org/10.3362/1756-3488.18-00010

Schwarz, M., Knoop, R. and Elffers, J. (2016) *A sustainist lexicon: Seven entrees to recast the future: Rethinking design heritage*. Amsterdam: Architectura and Natura Press.

Serrano-Tovar, T. and Giampietro, M. (2013) Multi-scale integrated analysis of rural Laos: Studying metabolic patterns of land uses across different levels and scales. *Land Use Policy*, 36, pp. 155–170.

Shove, E. and Walker, G. (2014) What is energy for? Social practice and energy demand. *Theory, Culture and Society*, 31, pp. 41–58. https://doi.org/10.1177/0263276414536746

Spiller, M. and Agudelo, C. (2011) Mapping diversity of urban metabolic functions: A planning approach for more resilient cities. *Proceedings of the 5th AESOP Young Academics Network Meeting, February 15–18, 2011 2011, Delft*. Delft: Delft University.

Steen, M. (2011) Tensions in human-centred design. *Co-Design*, 7 (1), pp. 45–60. https://doi.org/10.1080/15710882.2011.563314

UN (2012) *2011 UN-water GLAAS country survey: Raw output of written comments provided by country respondents* [Internet]. World Health Organisation. Available from: <www.who.int/water_sanitation_health/glaas/2011_glaas_country_survey.pdf> [Accessed 7 October 2019].

UN DESA (2009) *2007 demographic yearbook: Fifty-ninth issue*. New York: United Nations Department of Economic and Social Affairs, United Nations.

2 Remembering energy pasts

Situated practices and historic changes

In order to provide a situated understanding of changing energy practices in Kartong, this chapter offers a historic perspective based on biographic semi-structured interviews with elders in the community. These were largely carried out together with Dr Mary Greene from the National University of Ireland in Galway[1] and funded through the Shape Energy Research Design Challenge (https://shapeenergy.eu/). Interviews focused on men and women between 50 and 100 years of age who were asked to reflect on changing energy practices from their childhoods onwards.

Locating Kartong and its people

Kartong is located on the south coast of The Gambia across the border from the Casamance region of southern Senegal. To the north, Kartong land borders the town of Gunjur and the smaller settlements of Madina Salam and Berending sandwiched in between. It is surrounded by water on the remaining three sides including the Atlantic Ocean to the west and the Allahein (or Halahin) river to the east and south. Kartong is said to be one of the oldest communities in The Gambia and the first families that settled here included the Diaros and Sonkos. They were eventually followed by the Tourey, Manneh and Jabang families who remained and were joined by the Mannehs and the Jabangs. These went on to form four *kabilo* or clan areas named Tourey Kunda, Manneh Kunda, Jabang Kunda-Bah and Jabang Kunda-Ring.[2] The oldest male elders from each kabilo along with the *alkalo*, the head of a Gambian community, form the traditional leadership. Thomson (2012) suggests that the alkaloship has its origins in pre-colonial structures but was "significantly redefined" in the colonial era. In the decades following independence from the United Kingdom in 1965, so-called Village Development Committees (VDCs) were established as more formalised local government bodies across the Gambia. Officially, these were introduced by the Department of Community Development in the 1980s to encourage participation of communities in development processes (Davis et al., 1994; Schroeder, 1997). In Kartong, the traditional leadership structure was subsequently integrated into the local VDC.[3]

The kabilos also loosely represent different ethnic groups. For example, Tourey ethnically belongs to Mandinka people whereas Jabang is traditionally Jola. Minority groups that settled in Kartong over time include Wolof and Karoninka. The latter are related to the Jola and came to The Gambia from Casamance, thereby contributing to close cross-border relationships. Furthermore, increased numbers of Balanta settled in Kartong and Madina Salam as a result of the Guinea Bissau decade long war for independence from Portugal which ended in 1974.

Due to the ethnic diversity found locally, several languages are spoken but Mandinka is the most common language in Kartong and The Gambia as a whole. Over time many locals have been brought up without the ability to speak their ethnic tongue in a wider process that has been referred to as 'Mandigization' (Thomson, 2011).

Arguably the fluidity between ethnic identities, exacerbated by intermarriages and subsequent family ties, has contributed to religious plurality and tolerance in Kartong.[4] As one man explains, his father converted from Christianity to Islam which means both religions exist in the wider family (Schiffer, 2016a). Interwoven with the two major religions, heterodox and traditional practices have also shaped daily life. Perhaps most famously this includes practices surrounding *Folonko* – the sacred crocodile pool – where female elders carry out rituals to help people with fertility problems and other issues (Skramstad, 2008; Thomson, 2015).

Historic food practices

When energy is defined as the ability to do work, the most basic source of fuel enabling physical labour and participation in everyday life is food. In the past, families in Kartong relied almost entirely on the land surrounding the settlement for their livelihoods. "Actually, food was not our problem," recalls a woman in her mid-50s about her childhood. She continues: "In those days we have a lot of water and we have a lot of rice" (P2).[5] Others agree that because there was no shortage of rain people "get a lot from the farm and the *faros*," referring to local rice fields (P3; P4).[6,7] Alongside rice, people commonly grew *coose* (digitaria exilis), *findo* (millet) and maize, as well as groundnuts (P5).[8,9]

Staple crops such as rice were grown during the rainy season and vegetables during the dry season. In turn, this shaped food growing and consumption practices throughout the year. A woman who moved to Kartong in the late 1970s recalls that when she arrived, other women trained her in vegetable gardening. Where she grew up the focus was on growing crops during the rainy season and people did not depend on vegetable gardening in the dry season (P3).[10] In Kartong, however, the climate was suitable for growing vegetables though her arrival also coincided with the 'vegetable garden boom' in which women across the country started to convert land for crops during the dry season (Schroeder, 1997).

Prior to being stored for longer periods of time, vegetables and grains were dried under the sun and could so be used year round. In contrast, fish or meat consumed at household level was commonly preserved for shorter periods. As one respondent describes, when his mother worked on the rice fields, he would buy fish, clean it and then steam it over the fire so it would keep until the next day. Others also remember that fish was 'kept on the fire' to preserve it for several days, or immediately washed in the river, boiled and dried (P2, P11).[11,12] It should however be noted that smoking or salt-curing fish was also practised.

Some used fresh lime as seasoning for fish or collected salt from the salt flats along the river. Similarly, honey to sweeten dishes was sourced locally and oils were derived from groundnuts or palm trees (P2; P4).[13,14,15] Palm trees were also used by the Christian minority to engage in 'tapping' and produce palm wine (P2).[16]

The environment was rich in providing a diverse range of food resources and there was little need to buy produce. Food growing and consumption practices were largely based on a circular energy metabolism, where "we grow what we eat and we eat what we grow" (P4, also P6).[17,18]

However, while most respondents talked of abundant food resources produced locally, a man in his 50s recalled the painful memories of relatives skipping meals during the rainy season. "I can fully remember my dad would go to the bush without food" (P10).[19] He described that women prepared an early lunch to take to their families working on the rice fields who had not had breakfast, while they themselves skipped meals they had prepared for their husbands and children. A man several decades older remembers that his family sometimes gathered bush fruit to bridge seasonal food shortages. These were heated over the fire and eaten together with milk (P7).[20]

The inability to grow sufficient food to sustain one's family had a stigma attached to it: "Even if your rice that you grow is finished, you are ashamed of going to the shop to buy rice in a bag" (P4).[21] Similarly: "In those days everybody is ashamed that there is hunger in this home" (P2).[22] People consumed what they worked for and those who were unable to feed their family were thought to be lazy. Subsequently, "you are ashamed to go and buy this . . . *toubab*[23] rice" available from local shops which was also seen as low quality, associated with bad smells and thought to be contaminated (P2, P4).[24,25] Therefore, while it was possible to purchase rice, this was done in secret, as not to feel or cause embarrassment: "If you are going to do it you are going to arrange with the shopkeeper very late in the night. You go and pick it" (P4).[26]

Yet, strong social ties also compensated for household food shortages as the extended community looked after families or visitors who were unable to feed themselves: Families shared their surplus rice with 'strangers' or households that had not managed to produce enough for themselves. Again, this was done in secret and food was taken to a family compound at night, to avoid causing shame and embarrassment: "we want to be equal, we don't want to demote anyone" (P2).[27]

Furthermore, it would be erroneous to think that the predominately circular system of food production existed entirely independent from wider international trade networks. This is demonstrated by the practices surrounding brewing and drinking *ataya*, a tea prepared from imported Chinese leaves and brewed together with a large quantity of sugar resulting in a bitter, yet sweet taste. Ataya is brewed over a lengthy period of time whilst socialising with others. One respondent recalls that as a child he used to visit a male relative who was "an ataya addict." "I grow under him so I think this is also why I develop the addiction of drinking ataya" (P4).[28] Another man claims "I was born, found my dad drinking ataya and I trained, brewing ataya in my compound here" (P10).[29] This shows how even in the past Kartong and the wider Gambia participated in what Wright (2010) describes as 'world systems' of trade, though overall the emphasis was on local production and subsistence.

Similar to tea leaves, sugar had to be bought into the community, though it was not expensive and shopkeepers often handed it out as a present to good customers. People hardly carried cash in those days and tended to rely on bartering instead. A female respondent explains that one could pound rice, take it to the shop and swap it for sugar. Furthermore, grains could be swapped for smoked fish, and one could obtain small amounts of money needed in exchange for goods such as groundnuts and palm kernels (P2).[30] While respondents of both genders recall bartering, interviews suggest a gendered dimension in that men put greater emphasis on the availability of money. This is likely associated with cash crops such as groundnuts that were typically grown by men. In contrast, the aforementioned female respondent suggests that when formal education started and school fees were introduced, people became more reliant on monetary income: "When I have something I have to sell it in order to solve my problem instead of giving that thing to some[one] for mercy" (P2).[31]

Those who had livestock – including sheep, goats and cattle – made use of the milk or swapped animal products in exchange for extra help with their fields. With the absence of bank accounts, livestock formed a kind of security which could be exchanged against goods, money or services in case of an emergency. Jaitner et al. (2001, p. 106) suggest that reasons for keeping goats or sheep include "sales (cash income), insurance against crop failure, socio-cultural and ceremonial purpose and charity, manure and as exchange for cattle." For example, when getting married, a groom's family was likely expected to give the family of the bride a sheep as part of the marriage arrangement. The bride's family would not consume the meat but instead keep the sheep as an asset for their daughter to be sold in case of emergencies (P6).[32]

In the past, everyday life revolved around living off the land. One respondent recalls that a small number of people in the community, including his uncle, received animal-drawn tools to plough fields through an agricultural co-operative.[33] However, this was an exception. Rather than relying on animals, children were an integral part of the family workforce at a time when livelihoods relied almost exclusively on manual labour. "[The more] children you have behind you, [the] wider the land you till" (P10).[34] In turn, this required women to bear many children.

However, as Thomson (2015, p. 36) observes: "Infertility is unfortunately common and a serious calamity in The Gambia." To an extent, a lack of children could be compensated through wider family ties in which children grew up in polygamous or specifically polygynous marriages with up to four wives. Furthermore, it was not uncommon for children to grow up with relatives. As one woman explains, she was given to a childless aunt as a baby (P5).[35] In fact, children were looked after by the wider community. "In those days we don't know our real mothers . . . because all mother are equal and any mother can beat you" (P2).[36] People respected each other, respected elders and conformed to established social conventions and patriarchal structures. In this context, girls and boys grew up being trained for their specific gender roles.

Gendered roles and responsibilities

At a young age, girls' chores included looking after babies, washing basins and sweeping the house. This enabled their mothers to focus on main duties including farming or cooking (P4; P9).[37,38] When girls grew older they were trained to take on more responsibilities including cooking, fetching water and pounding rice (P8).[39] As one female respondent recalls, in the evening she would pound grains ready for the next day, then wash out the basins before cooking dinner. By the time she was done with her domestic chores, it was time to sleep (P5).[40] Similarly, a woman approaching 100 years of age says that what she remembers as a child is that she worked (P12).[41] When she was around twelve, she transferred to another compound in Kartong to live with a relative who could not have children of her own. She cooked, fished for oysters in the river and worked on the rice fields during the rainy season. She stayed in the compound until she got married in her early twenties.

Likewise, another woman explains that she transferred to her grandmother's place at around the age of ten. She helped her with vegetable gardening and carried out chores around the house including cooking and washing clothes (P9).[42] Soap for cleaning basins and washing was derived from the by-products of local palm oil production and water came from local wells (P5).[43] To iron clothes women used flat heavy irons that were placed into the fire to heat up. Those who owned two such irons could increase efficiency by heating one in the fire while the other was cooling down during ironing (P3).[44] Eventually, these were replaced with irons that contained hot charcoal.

In contrast, boys' lives differed greatly. While women and girls were engaged in chores throughout the year, the work of men and boys was concentrated during the rainy season. From around ten years of age boys were at home waiting for food to be ready to carry it to those working on the rice fields. At around fifteen they were trained to plough, preparing rice fields for their female counterparts who tended rice nurseries, before transplanting and finally harvesting the staple crop. As one male respondent recalls: "when it is rainy season you work from dusk til dawn," "that time seasons are separated, when it is time to work, [there is] no time to play" (P4).[45]

As one female respondent explains during the rainy season, age groups or *kafos* of boys and girls worked together to help each other's mothers or fathers on their fields. The boys will go "from father to father and we will go and transplant [rice] from mother to mother" (P2).[46] Similarly, a male respondent recalls: "[young] people were staying together and they work . . . in union" (P4).[47]

During the dry season boys fetched firewood for their mothers, but generally had more free time than girls. Boys did not have to go far to fetch firewood for cooking as the settlement finished around the school and one could collect firewood from the immediate environment, including the area around Folonko. They would also collect firewood from an area near the beach. There was a forest so thick that they would go in a group, afraid to encounter large snakes by themselves.

Other boys engaged in activities such as wrestling, football or hunting after the rice harvest was complete. If they caught a wild animal they would stay out in the bush and cook it for themselves (P4).[48] A respondent in his early fifties recalls that he and his friends would sometimes engage in local story-telling competitions or borrow a [cassette] tape and organise mixed-gender dances (P10).[49]

The above illustrates that traditionally, there was a strong gender dimension in relation to everyday household- and food-related practices, putting a larger burden on women and girls who had responsibilities related to physical work all year round. Socialisation into distinct male and female gender roles happened from a young age through to adolescence and into adulthood (Chant and Jones, 2005). However, there was a certain flexibility to deal with the lack of available female workforce in particular. Two male respondents in their fifties (P10)[50] and seventies (P11),[51] respectively, carried out both traditional boys' and girls' chores. They compensated for the fact they did not have any sisters. As such, they fetched firewood for their mothers and ploughed rice fields as they grew older; they also washed basins, pounded rice and cooked for the family.

Changing mobility

On land, most local journeys around Kartong and visits to the relatively nearby settlements of Gunjur, Sifoe or Sanyang were done on foot (P4; P5).[52,53] A woman recalls that she occasionally walked around 10 km to Gunjur (P5).[54] When she was highly pregnant with one of her sons she walked there, stayed the night, walked back to Kartong the following day and immediately gave birth. Another respondent remembers that he traveled to Gunjur and other nearby communities for football matches in his youth (P10).[55] People also journeyed on foot to the capital Banjul (formerly Bathurst) approximately 65 km to the north whilst carrying 20 L barrels of palm oil or other goods to trade. Again, they stopped overnight along the way (P2).[56] However, for the majority of people to travel such distances was uncommon and most *Kartonkas*[57] did not journey much outside of the village (P5).[58] Especially children were not often taken outside of the community (P4).[59]

People recall that during their childhoods bicycles were rare (P8).[60] A woman in her late fifties suggests: "If you see a bicycle with somebody you know this one is very rich" (P2).[61] A respondent two decades older remembers only one man having a bicycle in Kartong when he was a child. Around the 1960s bicycles started to become more common and were used by boys and men but not by girls and women (P11).[62]

Motorised transport was also limited. According to one respondent, the first motorcycle in Kartong was extremely noisy and belonged to a Kartonka who had received a degree in agriculture from a university in Nigeria and had to travel frequently for work. People in the community called it *Pitipiti-bah* – the first part comprised of an onomatopoeia mimicking the sound, the second meaning big. The motorbike could be heard long before it reached the community and children would chase the sound in hope of seeing it moving (P10).[63]

One man interviewed recalls that there were truck drivers employed by "large commercials" to operate in villages where they lived (P4).[64] More specifically, there was a rich businessman engaged in the groundnut trade who was based in Gunjur. He owned several trucks with wooden carriers. People would sell their harvest to him and the vehicles were used to collect groundnuts from people's fields and drive them to a depot in Banjul (P10).[65]

In the early 1970s, there were very few people in Kartong who owned a car but there was one man who operated a taxi that left early in the morning to travel to Banjul and return late at night (P2; P4; P5).[66,67,68] "To own a car that time or to own transport was not actually a concept in the community, otherwise many people can afford [it]" (P4).[69] Another respondent suggests that when motorised vehicles were uncommon, individual car ownership was not encouraged because dependence on that individual to provide transport for relatives and friends would be enormous (P10).[70] As such, social ties that would have enabled access to faster modes of transport for some actually discouraged individual car ownership.

Later in the decade and into the early 1980s transport practices began to change with the construction of a road linking Kartong to Gunjur (P4, P11).[71,72] The number of (male) drivers increased, improving travel to and from Kartong.[73] However, during the rainy season travel on motorised transport remained a challenge due to frequent inundation (P11).[74] Following the 1994 coup d'état in which Yahya Jammeh seized power, road infrastructure improved further and more people started owning private vehicles, though this continued to be associated with privilege and many still had to walk considerable distances (P10).[75] As one man remembers:

> it will take you 8–10 h to travel from Brikama to Kartong in those days. It was very difficult. Sometimes you struggle from Brikama to get to Gunjur. From Gunjur to Kartong you don't think of a vehicle. You walk on foot.
>
> (Schiffer, 2016b, p. 54)[76]

Over time, improved road networks, private car ownership and increased availability of minivan *bush taxis* started to enable people to commute weekly or daily to work in urban areas to the north. However, improved road infrastructure also led to a creeping dependence on fossil fuels for motorised vehicles which were bought into the community from the petrol stations in Gunjur or Brikama. This marked the beginning of an increasingly linear energy metabolism for transport connecting Kartong with other places in The Gambia and beyond.

Though partly influenced by a number of factors, including the introduction of new technologies and infrastructural developments, past changes in transport practices were also shaped by gender, political and seasonal dynamics. Several stages of road construction paved the way for a gradual increase in motorised transport, less and less hampered by inundation during the rainy season. Transport changes impacted more directly on men who adopted the use of bicycles or learnt to drive motorised vehicles when these became available in the community.

However, road infrastructure also enabled repeated periods of commercial mineral sand extraction which first began in the 1990s (Schiffer, 2016b). This led to a radically changed area of land located between the settlement of Kartong and the Atlantic coast. Vast sand dunes that once served as a natural barrier between buildings and the coastal shores were replaced with depressions, some of which became inundated with water and created habitats for birds, crocodiles and mosquitoes. In the process women's vegetable gardens were adversely affected (Manneh, 2009). As one woman explains: before the mining began, she grew vegetables in a garden nested between the sand dunes but the mining forced her to relocate. She feels the land she uses now is not as fertile and roaming cows threaten her crops (P8).[77] For vegetable gardeners in Kartong, the construction of what is known as the Kombo Coastal Road has been a double-edged sword. Many have been affected by the mining that would not have been viable without the road but at the same time its construction improved access to urban markets where they could sell their produce.

The majority of daily activities in the settlement were land based and so was associated mobility. However, the waters which surround Kartong also played an increasingly important role. A woman engaged in oyster fishing recalls that those who collected oysters, cockles or crabs would use locally carved boats and paddles. Larger boats were available to transport fish and agricultural crops such as rice or groundnuts that were collected in baskets from family land and then moved along the Allahein. Boats were also used to cross the border to Casamance on two points along the river (P2).[78]

She recalls that Senegalese fishermen started fishing in the Atlantic Ocean near Kartong in the 1970s. They introduced motorised fishing boats that could both be used along the Allahein river but also cope with the open sea. Subsequently, a family settled in what became a hamlet known as Cocotown. They started fishing for *bonga*, a type of fish which that was smoked to preserve it and sold to the provinces where there was no access to fresh fish.

Over time, fishermen had to adapt to physical changes in the structure of the Allahein river. Comparing satellite images, the river mouth has shifted approximately 2.2 km south in three and a half decades due to a 'depositional strand plain' (Jallow et al., 1996; Google Earth Pro, 1984, 2018). Exacerbated during falling tides, boats have had to learn to navigate the additional passage to the 'river side,' where smoke houses to preserve bonga are located.

Sharing information

Prior to other means of mobility becoming available, messages were carried on foot (P5; P7).[79,80] Within Kartong, a type of drum called *tabula* which was normally located at the mosque or the compound of the alkalo would sound to let people know they had to gather to find out important information. One participant recalls that the Karoninka used to blow a type of horn to alert people that labour was required in the bush or that lunch was ready. When people heard the sound of the horn "they say Jarjou Kunda is eating" (P2).

Over time the use of bicycles became the preferred method for physically passing on information – for example alerting people that there was a funeral (P4; P8; P11).[81,82,83] However, one respondent recalls that when there was only one man in Kartong who owned a bicycle people felt ashamed to ask for help with transport. They would approach the man usually at night and in secret asking to borrow it (P11).[84] This changed with increased numbers of bicycles becoming available, though as a sign of respect, elders continued to visit the owners in person, state their case and ask to borrow the bicycle (P4, P8).[85,86] Another respondent says she was lucky because her relative was the alkalo and therefore given a bicycle.[87] Many would borrow it to send boys to pass on information verbally or by letter. In other parts of The Gambia passing communication was arguably easier. One man who moved to Kartong said that he grew up in Lower Baddibu where people used donkeys and horses to get around and spread news (P13).[88,89]

People recall that there was no radio in the community until around 1965, when The Gambia became independent from the United Kingdom. Radio Gambia was launched and obituaries could be announced (P11).[90,91] One man recalls that his father owned a radio and people would gather round it to listen to the news but the fact that this "small box can speak" was also a novel attraction (P14).[92] Another respondent remembers: "When I was a child at the age of 8, 9 to 10, there were few radios. Very few radios, very few radios and there were no newspapers, no, no" (P4).[93] He recalls the establishment of a prominent newspaper called *The Nation* by Gambian journalist Charles Dixon Colley but newspapers were hard to come by in Kartong and illiteracy rates were high (The Independent, 2003). This meant reports on the radio were more accessible. Over time radios became more popular in the community and people relied on them for information. However, they also had ongoing expenses associated with them, including paying for batteries and maintenance. Another man suggests that his father was an early adaptor of this technology and people would converge around his radio to listen to the one o'clock news (P10).[94] Information was broadcast in English, the official language of The Gambia even after independence, as well as Mandinka and Wolof, the most commonly spoken ethnic tongues (Juffermans, 2013). Later, other local languages were added to the broadcast (P10).[95] Interestingly, around the 1981 attempted coup d'état the national radio station was seized by those involved in the failed overthrow of the government to disseminate their propaganda (P10; Sallah, 1990).[96,97] However, this was short lived.

There were no televisions but some people traveled to cinema halls that had opened in the large cities of Banjul, Serrekunda and Brikama and would mainly show Indian and Chinese films (P10; P13).[98] Eventually cinema halls opened up in other parts of the country including neighbouring Gunjur. One respondent suggests that these were the predecessors of what later became so-called 'video clubs,' a local form of cinema powered by off-grid diesel generators (P4).[99]

Similar to transport, the communication sector saw significant infrastructural development under Jammeh, including the launch of the country's first television station and the development of a mobile phone network (Munro and Schiffer, 2019; Harvey and Sturges, 2010). However, freedom of speech became increasingly suppressed.

Prior to the availability of mobile phones, some communities including Kartong were connected via landlines. Initially only a few compounds had the service installed which they shared with their neighbours. These in turn would pass on the number to friends and relatives. The pressure on individuals who had landlines in their compounds to pass on messages or make appointments for other people to receive phone calls was somewhat mitigated through the introduction of telecentres. These were commercial entities that provided access for those who could not afford the monthly subscription fee of a landline and wanted to pay for single calls instead – similar to internet cafes that were yet to arrive (P10).[100] One respondent, who moved to Kartong when she got married, remembers that there was a telecentre in Gunjur. It was not possible to pass messages directly to the community where she was from but via another town that had a phone box (P3).[101] However, before landline usage could spread more widely, it was superseded by the introduction of the mobile phone which became available around the year 2000. Over time changes in available communication technologies increasingly connected people beyond the boundaries of Kartong.

Lighting methods

Previously, the majority of people in Kartong used an improvised version of a kerosene lamp. These were commonly constructed from empty Ovaltine tins with a hole drilled in the lid to feed a string through. The latter would soak up the flammable liquid held inside (P2; P5, P10, P11).[102,103,104,105] The lamps caused a lot of smoke and left black marks on walls and ceilings when they burned. In contrast, so-called 'hurricane' lamps were seen as more comfortable because the glass cover reduced smoke emissions and provided a better quality of light. It was therefore preferred to the make-shift systems of light production (P10).[106] A female respondent explains that there was a large hurricane lamp hanging in the middle of the *bum-bah*, the traditional bedroom shared by women and children in her compound (P3).[107] However, few in the community could afford this type of lamp.

Kerosene was available from shops or roadside stalls that would bulk buy larger quantities in Gunjur and resell a cup at a price: "if you have money you buy, if you don't you bring rice and exchange that to [kerosene]" (P2).[108] Alternatively, those who could not afford kerosene (or candles) placed wood fires inside the house with people huddling round to provide lighting and warmth (P2, P11).[109,110] One respondent remembers when there was a shortage of kerosene at home, her mother created a fire in the middle of the house where everybody would settle in the room ready to sleep. She used water to wet the floor around the fire to keep them safe. However, when there was money, the family used kerosene instead (P8).[111]

Some people collected and burned the large stones of a fruit called *tambakulo* which kept their heat and caused less smoke (P3; P11).[112,113] The fruit was especially used during the cold season, associated with the cool and dusty winds known as Harmattan blowing from the Sahara Desert. Fires were lit outside until the smoke reduced and then transferred indoors to heat the home (P3).[114] Children gathered round indoor fires and their mothers told stories. As one woman recalls: "those are our televisions, we listen to those stories" (P2).[115] However, she also remembers fondly that: "when there is moonlight . . . then we go out and play, we enjoy. You see the children shouting in the street."

While respondents did not report illness or accidents, the risks to heath when burning biomass and using kerosene fuels (especially to women and children) are well documented (Mills, 2016).[116] Over time, kerosene became increasingly difficult to access and the use of candles evolved into the dominant methods for lighting. In turn, candles were eventually replaced by or used in parallel to battery powered torches and lamps.

At household level, technological change, economic buying power and availability of resources shaped lighting practices over time. Lighting resources became increasingly dependent on a variety of imported technologies, energy carriers (such as batteries) and fuels. However, circular systems based on locally sourced biomass prevailed, or at least supplemented the increasingly linear metabolism, especially when imported fuels such as kerosene were not available.

Finally, national political events at least temporarily brought about drastic changes regarding lighting infrastructure at community level. The unstable political situation around the time of the 1994 coup d'état impacted negatively on businesses operating in The Gambia and in some cases led to their closure. Long-standing employees of one such business were compensated with equipment that was no longer needed. This included a technician from Kartong who was given a large diesel generator that was too big to be used domestically. He decided to offer it to the community to generate electricity for street lighting. One respondent who retells the story suggests it was an opportunity for Kartong to have such a system at a time when even Serrekunda, the most prominent urban area in The Gambia, had only limited electricity access (P4).[117] However, fuel and maintenance costs were to be covered by the community, which proved to be challenging and the project eventually collapsed. Arguably, this highlights limited capabilities to manage such community-owned systems at the time and demonstrates the financial burden of fossil fuel dependence to deliver access to modern energy services such as electricity for street lighting.

Shaping energy practices

This chapter has demonstrated that socio-cultural (e.g. gender), environmental, economic, technological and political dimensions have shaped changing energy practices of Kartong in the past. It has thereby also illustrated the need for a more holistic understanding of metabolic processes in energy systems in which different practices such as communication and mobility are closely linked.

Elders in the community recall a time when the local energy metabolism was essentially circular in terms of food, mobility, lighting and communication practices. Changing seasons, in particular the dry and rainy seasons and corresponding food growing cycles significantly defined everyday life and practices over the course of a year. Locally sourced firewood was the predominant cooking fuel, also used to preserve animal-based proteins, heat homes and provide domestic lighting. People 'grew what they ate' relying on the land around them for food and other resources to sustain daily life. In this context of subsistence, goods were often exchanged directly through bartering.

At home and on the fields, practices in Kartong relied heavily on physical labour and activities were for the most part divided along clearly defined gender roles, with girls and women carrying out day-to-day household chores all year round. Strong family and friendship networks made the community more resilient. Where necessary, food resources, access to communication technologies and even children were given to others to ensure the overall wellbeing of the wider family and community at large.

Over time, new technologies became available, which in turn became increasingly reliant on imported energy carriers and fuels. For example, obtaining information became easier with the introduction of battery powered radios. Similarly, kerosene was used to provide household lighting though this was eventually replaced by candles and electric lamps which like the radio relied on batteries that had to be bought into the community. Diesel generators became more common to power services such as video clubs, and the fishing industry started to use motorised boats to access the Atlantic Ocean. However, the biggest shift towards fossil fuels is arguably associated with improvements in road infrastructure, which is linked to a changing political landscape that enabled a growing use of motorised vehicles to travel to and from Kartong. With that local practices began to shift towards a more linear energy metabolism. Furthermore, the increasing demand for energy imports also contributed to a growing need for a monetary-based economy. Some argue increasing individual and household need for cash reduced people's willingness to share resources without getting something in return. Here, cash crops such as groundnuts provided a major source of income. It has been suggested that in the wider Gambian context, a growing emphasis on agricultural income generation meant "women were further relegated to producing food crops while men focused on cash crops for export. Where relative gender equality or matrilineal relations existed, patrilineality ensued. And where relative food selfsufficiency existed, food dependence, especially of rice, took root" (Saine, 2012, p. 26).

Notes

1 Dr Greene has since been appointed as Assistant Professor in the Environmental Policy Group at Wageningen University, The Netherlands.
2 *Kunda* means compound and refers here to the compound of the respective (extended) family it belongs to. *Bah* translates as big or large and *ring* means

small, though it also indicates that Jabang-Kunda-Ring was settled after Jabang-Kunda-Bah.

3 Information about the governance structure of Kartong is largely based on a semi-structured interview with Sankung Sambou, former administrator of the Kartong Association of Responsible Tourism, which took place on 26 October 2010.
4 Ibid.
5 Participant 2, interviewed by author and M. Greene, Kartong, 6 January 2018.
6 Participant 3, interviewed by author, Kartong, 2 April 2018.
7 Participant 4, interviewed by author and M. Greene, Kartong, 4 January 2018.
8 Participant 5 (J. Jabang), interviewed by author and M. Greene, Kartong, 2 January 2018.
9 Groundnuts are The Gambia's most famous cash crop.
10 Ibid (n 6) Participant 3.
11 Ibid (n 5) Participant 2.
12 Participant 11, interviewed by author and M. Greene, Kartong, 6 January 2018.
13 Ibid (n 5) Participant 2.
14 Ibid (n 7) Participant 4.
15 It is worth noting that palm oil here is not associated with the devastating environmental degradation of industrial scale palm oil production.
16 Ibid (n 5) Participant 2.
17 Ibid (n 7) Participant 4.
18 Participant 6, interviewed by author and M. Greene, Kartong 6 January 2018.
19 Ibid.
20 Participant 7, interviewed by author, Kartong, 5 April 2018.
21 Ibid.
22 Ibid (n 5) Participant 2.
23 The word *toubab* translates into white person and toubab rice here refers to imported rice.
24 Ibid (n 5) Participant 2.
25 Ibid (n 7) Participant 4.
26 Ibid.
27 Ibid (n 5) Participant 2.
28 Ibid (n 7) Participant 4.
29 Participant 10, interviewed by author and M. Greene, Kartong, 2 January 2018.
30 Ibid (n 5) Participant 2.
31 Ibid.
32 Ibid (n 18) Participant 6.
33 Ibid (n 29) Participant 10.
34 Ibid.
35 Ibid (n 8) Participant 5.
36 Ibid (n 5) Participant 2.
37 Ibid (n 7) Participant 4.
38 Participant 9, interviewed by author and M. Greene, Kartong, 4 January 2018.
39 Participant 8, interviewed by author, Kartong 6 April 2018.
40 Ibid (n 8) Participant 5.
41 Participant 12, interviewed by author and M. Greene, Kartong, 1 January 2018.
42 Ibid (n 38) Participant 9.
43 Ibid (n 8) Participant 5.
44 Ibid (n 6) Participant 3.

45 Ibid (n 7) Participant 4.
46 Ibid (n 5) Participant 2.
47 Ibid (n 7) Participant 4.
48 Ibid.
49 Ibid (n 29) Participant 10.
50 Ibid.
51 Ibid (n 12) Participant 11.
52 Ibid (n 7) Participant 4.
53 Ibid (n 8) Participant 5.
54 Ibid.
55 Ibid (n 29) Participant 10.
56 Ibid (n 5) Participant 2.
57 Kartonka refers to a person from Kartong.
58 Ibid (n 8) Participant 5.
59 Ibid (n 7) Participant 4.
60 Ibid (n 39) Participant 8.
61 Ibid (n 5) Participant 2.
62 Ibid (n 12) Participant 11.
63 Ibid (n 29) Participant 10.
64 Ibid (n 7) Participant 4.
65 Ibid (n 29) Participant 10.
66 Ibid (n 5) Participant 2.
67 Ibid (n 7) Participant 4.
68 Ibid (n 8) Participant 5.
69 Ibid (n 7) Participant 4.
70 Ibid (n 29) Participant 10.
71 Ibid (n 7) Participant 4.
72 Ibid (n 12) Participant 11.
73 Whilst women could join transport, only men learnt to drive motorised vehicles.
74 Ibid (n 12) Participant 11.
75 Ibid (n 29) Participant 10.
76 Interviewed by the author, Kartong, 25 April 2014.
77 Ibid (n 39) Participant 8.
78 Ibid (n 5) Participant 2.
79 Ibid (n 8) Participant 5.
80 Ibid (n 20) Participant 7.
81 Ibid (n 7) Participant 4.
82 Ibid (n 39) Participant 8.
83 Ibid (n 12) Participant 11.
84 Ibid.
85 Ibid (n 7) Participant 4.
86 Ibid (n 39) Participant 8.
87 Ibid (n 8) Participant 5.
88 Participant 13, interviewed by author and M. Greene, Kartong 6 January 2018.
89 In theory people were also able to send and receive mail from overseas through Gampost in Banjul though sending a letter and receiving a reply could take several months. It also required someone able to write either in English or Arabic. In The Gambia Arabic is mainly used in the context of Islamic religious practice (Igboanusi, 2013).
90 Radio Gambia was launched in 1962, three years before independence from the UK.

91 Ibid (n 12) Participant 11.
92 Participant 14, interviewed by author and M. Greene, Kartong 3 January 2018.
93 Ibid (n 7) Participant 4.
94 Ibid (n 29) Participant 10.
95 Ibid.
96 Ibid.
97 The attempted overthrow of the government occurred while then president Dawda Kairaba Jawara was on holiday to attend Lady Diana and Prince Charles' wedding in London (Whiteman, 2019).
98 Ibid (n 29) Participant 10.
99 Ibid (n 7) Participant 4.
100 Ibid (n 29) Participant 10.
101 Ibid (n 6) Participant 3.
102 Ibid (n 5) Participant 2.
103 Ibid (n 8) Participant 5.
104 Ibid (n 29) Participant 10.
105 Ibid (n 12) Participant 11.
106 Ibid (n 29) Participant 10.
107 Ibid (n 6) Participant 3.
108 Ibid (n 5) Participant 2.
109 Ibid.
110 Ibid (n 12) Participant 11.
111 Ibid (n 39) Participant 8.
112 Ibid (n 6) Participant 3.
113 Ibid (n 12) Participant 11.
114 Ibid (n 6) Participant 3.
115 Ibid (n 5) Participant 2.
116 This is not to say that there never were any health impacts or accidents. Over the years of visiting Kartong I have personally suffered from the effects associated with prolonged cooking in a semi-enclosed space, whilst observing women and children cough or complain about the discomforts caused by smoke. I have also come across several children with burns including one that fell into a wood fire used to provide lighting.
117 Ibid (n 7) Participant 4.

References

Chant, S. and Jones, G.A. (2005) Youth, gender and livelihoods in West Africa: Perspectives from Ghana and the Gambia. *Children's Geographies*, 3 (2), pp. 185–199. https://doi.org/10.1080/14733280500161602

Davis, D., Hulme, D. and Woodhouse, P. (1994) Decentralization by default: Local governance and the view from the village in the Gambia. *Public Administration and Development*, 14, pp. 253–269. https://doi.org/10.1002/pad.4230140303

Google Earth Pro V 7.3.2.5491 (2018) *Kartong, the Gambia, 13°04'15.99"N, 16°45'08.68"W, elevation 0M, eye alt 14.77, landsat/copernicus, 2019 CNES/airbus*, 28 October. [Accessed 6 March 2019].

Google Earth Pro V 7.3.2.5491 (1984) *Kartong, the Gambia, 13°04'15.99"N, 16°45'08.68"W, elevation 0M, eye alt 14.77, Landsat/Copernicus*, 31 December. [Accessed 6 March 2019].

Harvey, J. and Sturges, P. (2010) The cell phone as appropriate information technology: Evidence from the Gambia. *Information Development*, 26 (2), pp. 148–159. https://doi.org/10.1177/0266666910367866

Igboanusi, H. (2013) The English-only language education policy in the Gambia and low literacy rates. *Journal International Journal of Bilingual Education and Bilingualism*, 17 (5), pp. 558–569. https://doi.org/10.1080/13670050.2013.851642

The Independent (2003) Gambia: Dixon colley remembered. *The Independent/ All Africa* [Online], 20 January. Available from: <https://allafrica.com/stories/200301200168.html> [Accessed 4 October 2018].

Jaitner, J., Sowe, J., Secka-Njie, E. and Dempfle, L. (2001) Ownership pattern and management practices of small ruminants in the Gambia: Implications for a breeding programme. *Small Ruminant Research*, 40, pp. 101–108. https://doi.org/10.1177/0266666910367866

Jallow, P.J., Barrow, M.K.A. and Leatherman, S.P. (1996) Vulnerability of the coastal zone of the Gambia to sea level rises and development of response strategies and adaptation options. *Climate Research*, 6 (2), pp. 165–177. Available from: <www.jstor.org/stable/24865084>

Juffermans, K. (2013) Engaging with voices: Ethnographic encounters with the Gambian language-in-education policy. *Anthropology & Education Quarterly*, 44 (2), pp. 142–160. https://doi.org/10.1111/aeq.12012

Manneh, E.F. (2009) A plea from Kartong. *Daily Observer* [Online], 17 June. Available from: <http://archive.observer.gm/africa/gambia/article/a-plea-from-kartong> [Accessed 1 March 2016].

Mills, E. (2016) Identifying and reducing the health and safety impacts of fuel-based lighting. *Energy for Sustainable Development*, 30, pp. 39–50. https://doi.org/10.1016/j.esd.2015.11.002

Munro, P.G. and Schiffer (2019) Ethnographies of electricity scarcity: Mobile phone charging spaces and the recrafting of energy poverty in Africa. *Energy and Buildings*, 188–189 (April), pp. 175–183. https://doi.org/10.1016/j.enbuild.2019.01.038

Saine, A. (2012) *Culture and customs of Gambia*. Santa Barbara: Greenwood.

Sallah, T.M. (1990) Economics and politics in the Gambia. *The Journal of Modern African Studies*, 8 (4), pp. 621–648. Available from: <www.jstor.org/stable/160924>

Schiffer, A. (2016a) *Designers in international development: A reflection on designing Gambian energy futures* [PhD thesis]. Queen's University Belfast.

Schiffer, A. (2016b) Empowered, excited, or disenfranchised? Unveiling issues of energy access inequality and resource dependency in the Gambia. *Energy Research & Social Science*, 18 (August), pp. 50–61. https://doi.org/10.1016/j.erss.2016.04.011

Schroeder, R.A. (1997) "Re-claiming" land in the Gambia: Gendered property rights and environmental intervention. *Annals of the Association of American Geographers*, 87 (3), pp. 487–508. Available from: <www.jstor.org/stable/2564065>

Skramstad, H. (2008) *Making and managing femaleness, fertility and motherhood within an urban Gambian area* [PhD thesis]. Bergen: University of Bergen.

Thomson, S. (2015) To condone or to contest? Ethnic identity and religious architecture in the Gambia. In: Gharipour, M. ed. *Sacred precincts: The religious architecture of non muslim communities across the Islamic world.* Leiden: Brill, pp. 28–42.

Thomson, S. (2012) Developing a multiethnic ethos: Colonial legacies, national policies, and local histories converged in a Gambian village charter. *Studies in Ethnicity and Nationalism*, 12 (2), pp. 286–308. https://doi.org/10.1111/j.1754-9469.2012.01171.x

Thomson, S. (2011) Revisiting "mandingization" in coastal Gambia and casamance (Senegal): Four approaches to ethnic change. *African Studies Review*, 54 (2), pp. 95–121. https://doi.org/10.1353/arw.2011.0033

Whiteman, K. (2019) Sir Dawda Jawara obituary. *The Guardian* [Online], 30 August. Available from: <https://www.theguardian.com/world/2019/aug/30/sir-dawda-jawara-obituary> [Accessed 23 February 2020].

Wright, D.R. (2010) *The world and a very small place in Africa: A history of globalisation in Niumi, the Gambia.* 3rd ed. New York: M.E. Sharpe.

3 Delivering sustainable energy access

An exploration of leapfrogging in Kartong

In the past, Kartong was largely dependent on local resources such as food and firewood for meeting energy demands. This chapter explores the concept of leapfrogging in the context of delivering sustainable energy access by reflecting on these past changes of energy consumption practices. The term leapfrogging describes a process of jumping from older technologies to those further advanced and bypassing incremental technology upgrades in between. But what exactly does leapfrogging to 'modern energy' mean?

In its World Energy Outlook report, the International Energy Agency (IEA, 2017) uses the term 'modern energy' to describe access to electricity and clean cooking fuels at household level.[1] This focus is widely adopted in academic and technical literature (Makonese et al., 2018; Sambodo and Novandra, 2019; Pachauri et al., 2012). Murphy (2001), for example, explores the move from reliance on biomass, especially firewood and charcoal to renewable and more efficient models for electricity access as well as clean cooking stoves in East Africa. Similarly, Makonese et al. (2018) discuss the relationship between levels of access to modern energy for cooking and health. However, the IEA (2017) also acknowledges broader definitions of modern energy that include access to mechanical power used in agriculture and other economic activities as well as energy used for street lighting and public services such as healthcare or education.

To enable a more holistic understanding of changes in Kartong's energy metabolism a broader interpretation is also used here, including both household and community-wide services. In addition, it takes into account access to motorised transport to move goods and people over distances. While transport is generally not included in what constitutes modern energy, it is nonetheless increasingly understood as an important factor that shapes particularly rural poverty determining access to healthcare, markets, education and employment (Starkey and Hine, 2014; Sambodo and Novandra, 2019). As highlighted in the previous chapter, motorised transport in Kartong has historically also been the most significant contributor in a shift towards a linear energy system based on fossil fuels.

Leapfrogging to modern energy

Modern energy access is enshrined in the UN Sustainable Development Goals (SDGs) as Goal 7, which calls for 'access to affordable, reliable, sustainable and modern energy for all' (Wu and Wu, 2015). Generally speaking, developing countries are seen to rely on older technologies, having to play catch-up or develop access to technologies in the first place (Davison et al., 2000; You et al., 2019). It is commonly argued that those which are still developing first-time and more reliable access to modern energy services have an opportunity to bypass polluting fossil fuel technologies and go straight to implementing sustainable energy systems based on renewable sources (Harvey, 2015). The Secretary of the United Nations Framework Convention on Climate Change (UNFCCC) Patricia Espinosa (2018) recently asserted that some African countries will be able to "leapfrog the carbon-intense development" commonly associated with industrialisation, "and truly begin building low-carbon, resilient societies." Similarly, former secretary general of the United Nations (UN) Kofi Annan has stated that, "African nations do not have to lock into developing high-carbon old technologies; we can expand our power generation and achieve universal access to energy by leapfrogging into new technologies that are transforming energy systems across the world" (APP, 2015, p. 11).

Modern energy access is widely seen as a key driver to help meet wider development objectives (Bhattacharyya, 2012; Sambodo and Novandra, 2019). Therefore, "leapfrogging in Africa has a potential to help speed up the process of development using advanced systems" (Assefa, 2011, p. 4).

Furthermore, leapfrogging to renewable energy provides an opportunity to speed up the delivery to energy access in the first place by using decentralised renewable structures, which means countries have the potential to save infrastructural costs such as transmission lines (Batinge et al. 2019; Kumar, 2015).

Exploring leapfrogging through a historic lens

In Kartong the previously mentioned community street lighting initiative which was implemented around the time of the 1994 coup d'état, is an example of jumping to an advanced lighting system. For a brief period of time it provided unprecedented access to modern energy in the form of communal lighting that was unable to be delivered by commercial or national government initiatives anytime soon. Unfortunately, this lighting initiative followed a linear energy metabolism relying on costly and imported fossil fuels, which contributed to the failure of the project.

In a domestic context, insights shared by elders in Kartong clearly document that lighting practices did not leapfrog from non-electric lighting to lamps powered by solar or other forms of renewable electricity either. People practised several forms of non-electric lighting methods which include the use of indoor wood fires, candles and makeshift kerosene lamps, all of which also contribute to poor indoor air quality. These were superseded by and in some cases used in parallel to battery powered torch lamps.

Similarly, Kartong did not leapfrog from a total absence of telecommunication to mobile phones. This is in conflict to the way leapfrogging is often perceived in developing world contexts. The assumption is that it provides a method for overcoming the digital divide regarding access to information and communication technologies (ICTs) between developing and industrialised countries (Steinmueller, 2008; James, 2014; Raja and Christiaensen, 2017). However, while landlines were never that popular at household or community level, they did exist in Kartong and in other parts of The Gambia. Landline phones were superseded by mobile phones which are in turn being replaced by smart phone technology (see Chapter 4). With the introduction of smart phones going forward, it is easier to argue that people have leapfrogged to social media platforms and digital news, thereby bypassing print media which was never widely accessible in Kartong. Yet in terms of making calls, ICT leapfrogging is only occurring and subsequently benefitting late adopters in the community who have incidentally missed a technological step (Davison et al., 2000).

Reflecting on past changes regarding mobility between Kartong and other parts of the country and beyond, the village has become increasingly dependent on fossil fuels to power motorised transport. Without a viable alternative this suggests the community is on a path to being locked into a fossil fuel-based system moving forward.

It should also be noted that the coastal zone in Kartong falls within what is known as the Tourism Development Area (TDA) which is an 800-metre-wide strip that runs along the coast from Kotu to Kartong and was created under the Town and Country Planning Act of 1972 (Mitchell and Faal, 2006). For many years, tourism developments along the TDA were limited to its northern part, due to the lack of tarred roads. With the construction of the Kombo Coastal Road a number of small tourism resorts were set up along the Kartong coast from the late 1990s onwards. Tourism is a major economic activity in The Gambia and Kartong promotes responsible tourism developments that provide economic benefit to the community as well as preservation of the natural environment through the Kartong Association for Responsible Tourism, which was established in 2005.

Nonetheless, increased tourism from Europe also further extends the reliance on fossil fuels associated with aviation to and from The Gambia in addition to overland transport to and from Kartong.[2] Some have previously suggested that countries which are still developing local transport infrastructure could leapfrog to electric vehicles such as buses (Goldemberg, 1998). In turn, that electricity would have to be derived from renewable sources for it to replace reliance on fossil fuels. This would require reliable access to sufficient electricity to be available, ideally before motorised transport becomes widely used. However, as demonstrated in the previous chapter, that was not the case in Kartong. Instead motorised transport increased with improved roads but without the possibility of access to and therefore independent of electricity infrastructure.

Furthermore, the majority of motorised vehicles used in The Gambia are second-hand imports and maintenance standards vary greatly. Anybody who has spent time traveling on (bush) taxis has likely experienced delays due to poor maintenance. This includes instances of drivers having to pull over and use a stick to determine how much petrol is left in the tank or lie under the vehicle to adjust the brakes. Worse still, cars are known to regularly overheat and leave passengers rushing to exit the vehicle as it fills with smoke. Stories also abound of already frightening journeys at night without functioning headlamps interrupted as the axel snaps in two and the vehicle comes to a sudden standstill.

However, there is also capacity to continue fixing the predominately old European cars and minibuses to keep them on the road for longer. Tightening a loose fan belt or extracting, fixing and re-inserting a leaky radiator can be done with few tools in a relatively short period of time. It is no wonder that second-hand cars are so popular not just in The Gambia but across the West African region (Ezeoha et al., 2019). In contrast, maintenance and repair of newer models would require specialist skills and software.

It is however also argued that industrialised countries are in fact 'exporting pollution' by selling second-hand cars to developing nations (Edwards, 2017). Charitable endeavours such as the 'Plymouth-Banjul' challenge are just the tip of the iceberg. Annually, teams spend three weeks driving second-hand cars to be auctioned off at their destination to raise money for local causes. According to the organisers' website, which promotes challenges to a number of destinations:

> The world is becoming a dull and safe place ruled by health and safety bureaucrats and this applies to travel, too. However if you have a pile of excrement on your drive which needs scrapping and the local car scrap dump does not fill you with excitement, then buy some cable ties and gaffer tape, pack some food, fill your water bottle and jump in and go.
>
> (Dakar Challenge, n.d.)

Arguably, these imported second-hand cars are providing needed mobility at an affordable cost as well as funds for charity projects. However, they are also contributing to The Gambia being locked into a fossil-fuel–based transport economy of polluting, less-efficient and accident-prone vehicles (Boko, 2003; Essoh, 2013).

Technological capabilities for maintaining energy access

Without developing technological capabilities to maintain a higher standard of vehicles, let alone electric alternatives such as cars or buses, it seems difficult to suggest that The Gambia can leapfrog to more sustainable transport systems anytime soon.

The introductory chapter has already touched on the breadth of broken and poorly maintained technology around the country. There is undoubtedly a correlation between being able to install and maintain infrastructure and having the capability to leapfrog or even incrementally shift to renewable technology. During a 2010 visit to the village of Berending which is located several kilometres off the Kombo Coastal Road north east of Kartong, a local man shared his motivation for being the first person in the community to obtain an off-grid solar photovoltaic installation:

> We are many in this family and I would spend a lot of money on candles and we have small, small children everywhere . . . we can't take the risk of keeping the candle in the house because they could cause fire . . . for safety I think it's better to use solar.
>
> (P15)[3]

This demonstrates the capability and willingness to save and invest in new domestic technologies at least by some people in rural communities.

The man's solar system included a charge controller, a small piece of important kit that regulates electric current flowing in and out of the battery. This in turn stores electricity generated by the solar panel used to power lights, charge mobile phones and even a television. Charge controllers like his are usually small boxes that include red, amber and green light emitting diodes (LEDs) to indicate the level of charge of the battery, based on a simple traffic light layout. However, initially, he was not aware of the importance of the charge controller which led to the breaking of several batteries. Moreover, during the time of the interview there was only one operational traffic light in The Gambia, which was located at the north-western end of Kairaba Avenue in Serrekunda, the largest urban centre in the country.[4] Many rural Gambians were not aware of traffic light systems and could therefore not relate to this as a reference point. The man and his brother had different opinions about what the LED indicators – in particular the red light – meant for the state of the battery and subsequent household consumption of electricity. The anecdote highlights the inadequacy of the one-size-fits-all approach whereby components are designed regardless of the socio-technical contexts in which they are deployed.

The brothers' initial lack of knowledge about the equipment is not an isolated case. In a nearby police station the charge controller was connected incorrectly and therefore not actually controlling the charge while it was missing altogether in a solar system in a Kartong household. This also highlights the need for technical capacity building to enable successful implementation, let alone leapfrogging to renewable energy technologies. It is common knowledge that, "the level of skills in The Gambia is not sufficient for the magnitude of the energy challenge" (Diop et al., 2014, p. viii). In a report assessing the readiness for renewable energy in The Gambia by the International Renewable Energy Agency (IRENA), a section clearly outlines the need to 'build stakeholder capacity' at different levels and voices concern over the current dependence on foreign experts (Singh et al., 2013, p. 66). The common approach to development which assumes that handing over gadgets or infrastructure to people "will suffice to leapfrog them into the technological world of economic opportunities" is no longer tenable as demonstrated here (Alzouma, 2005, p. 339). Instead, the role of education in the context of leapfrogging, especially in the power sector, is vital (Sarabhai and Vyas, 2017).

Fortunately, The Gambia is taking important steps to build relevant capacity. In January 2018, I attended a meeting with high-level national stakeholders which have since developed a renewable energy curriculum to build technical capacity within the country. However, it will take time before sufficient numbers of graduates will complete training to meet the country's energy access challenges.

In the meantime, electricity demand and dependence on fossil fuels continue to grow as the next chapter will show. The slow pace at which the technological capacity gap is being addressed lags far behind the demand for skills today.

Renewable energy is not enough

Let us assume for a moment that capacity to operate, install and maintain systems is available alongside adequate finance and policies. Leapfrogging to energy access based on renewable sources is arguably not enough if the intention is to transition to a socially just energy future, which is not necessarily a given by deploying renewable technology alone. There are plenty of examples from around the world where renewable energy developments, such as mega dams, have been associated with human rights abuse, have displaced local people and caused large-scale environmental degradation not dissimilar to infrastructure associated with fossil fuels (cf. Marriott and Minio-Paluello, 2012). The 2016 assassination of Berta Cáceres, an environmental activist in Honduras who had been fighting against the destructive Agua Zarca hydropower project, shocked the environmental campaign's world (Shoichet et al., 2016). There have also been long-standing plans to develop large-scale hydroelectric power in the Gambia River Basin. The aim is to construct an electricity network for The Gambia, Guinea, Guinea Bissau and Senegal with a dam located in the Senegalese part of the basin and another dam in central Guinea (Jarju, 2019).

Instead, we need to develop approaches that "guarantee access to modern energy services without marginalizing the poor" and particular segments of society such as women (Bazilian et al., 2011, p. 3).

The increasing shift to decentralised ownership and community energy models of renewable energy in Europe and other parts of the world is seen as a way to overcome established political economy structures and transition to more sustainable and equitable energy futures. Therefore, developing first-time access provides an opportunity to leapfrog not just fossil fuel technology but also the centralised oligopolies found in many parts of the industrialised world. Energy access could be delivered using renewable technologies and based on more decentralised and 'democratic' ownership models of energy generation, distribution and supply.

In Europe and the US, energy democracy is seen as a way to integrate "policies linking social justice and economic equity with renewable energy transitions" (Burke and Stephens, 2017). Here, community energy initiatives provide structures to ensure communities have access to and reap greater benefits from renewable energy sources.[5] In community energy, emphasis is put on people's (collective) participation in the energy market as 'prosumers' and as active citizens that are empowered often through local initiatives. Community energy can be defined through a number of shared characteristics including: "Ordinary people or citizens are involved in running the project through community groups"; "there is a co-operative, democratic or specifically non-corporate structure"; "there are tangible local benefits to people living or working close to projects" and "the profits go back to the community or are re-invested in other community energy schemes" (Schiffer, 2014, p. 4).[6]

So-called energy co-operatives are arguably the most common form of community energy in this context and people typically buy shares and so become members.[7] Co-operatives follow a number of rules including the one-member-one-vote principle. This stipulates that every member has the same decision-making power regardless of their individual (usually financial) contribution. However, community energy initiatives can be based on an array of different legal structures including ones which may not require individuals to contribute financially. Legal structures depend on the national policy context in which a project is based as well as the particular aims and values of the community energy group involved (Roberts et al., 2014).

In The Gambia it could be argued that community energy models would build on localised structures of the past in which a circular energy metabolism was supported by resources from the surrounding area and negotiated through sharing practices. Here, people acted as what can also be described as prosumers who produced as well as consumed traditional sources of energy such as firewood. In terms of leapfrogging to modern forms of energy, participation would suggest that Gambian 'non-sumers,' for lack of a better word, should skip the passive consumer step that has commonly been adapted in industrialised countries and become active prosumers in the process of adopting modern energy services such as electricity (Vansintjan, 2015).

Arguably distributed and 'democratic' access to electricity in underserved areas of West Africa is currently based on small diesel generators reliant on fossil fuels (Adhekpukoli, 2018). However, in The Gambia a renewable energy example actually exists. The Batokunku wind turbine (Figure 3.1), located approximately 30 km north of Kartong is a community-owned wind project that generates electricity which is distributed and supplied to households via a mini-grid (see Box 3.1). While the overall system only works in conjunction with national grid infrastructure,[8] the community of Batokunku was able to leapfrog to an electricity system largely powered by community-owned renewables.

Unlike co-operatives, the set-up of Batokunku is actually more akin to the Development Trust (DT) model found in Scotland in which a local enterprise (which can take a number of different legal structures) is appointed to act on behalf of the community to support local development and regeneration (Roberts et al., 2014). DTs are usually governed by a board, similar to the Batokunku VDC's energy sub-committee. Due to the fact that VDCs are an integral part of local governance across The Gambia, this could potentially be adapted in other parts of the country.

There is however limited wind potential along the Gambian coastline and a small number of other wind projects since have not been developed as community-owned structures. Challenges of replicability could potentially be overcome with technology that is more broadly applicable across the country, such as solar energy. Furthermore, the Batokunku project is fairly complex, linking generation, distribution and supply which could be too burdensome for other communities. Nonetheless, the Batokunku wind turbine serves as an important symbol, demonstrating the potential of delivering renewable energy access through decentralised ownership structures in the West African context.

Figure 3.1 Batokunku wind turbine

Box 3.1   Batokunku wind turbine

Background

The Batokunku wind turbine is the first grid-connected and community-owned wind installation in The Gambia and known as the first project of its kind in West Africa. The 150 kilowatt turbine was installed in 2008 to provide electricity to households in the settlement connected by a mini-grid (Manneh, 2013).

Set-up and finance

The system is also connected to national grid infrastructure and makes use of a Power Purchase Agreement with the National Water and Electricity Company (NAWEC) which enables the sale of excess electricity and to buy in additional power when needed.

The project, which uses a second-hand Danish turbine, was initiated and sponsored by a German engineer. It has contracted a Dutch engineering firm in neighbouring Tujering to look after ongoing maintenance.

The local VDC has set up an energy sub-committee. The latter is responsible for the day-to-day management of the system including the settling of household bills. People in Batokunku have access to the cheapest available grid electricity in The Gambia and pay just under 22% of the cheapest NAWEC tariff available. This is due to the comparatively high cost of fossil fuels on which the majority of NAWEC generation currently depends. As of June 2012 the local electricity tariff was Dalasi 2 (€0.02; $0.04) per kWh compared with the cheapest tariff offered by NAWEC of Dalasi 9.1(€0.16; $0.18) per kWh (PURA, n.d.).

While high-level stakeholders are addressing the technical capacity gap through the development of the aforementioned renewable energy curriculum, alternative ownership and associated financing models also require new skills to be developed for the specific context of Gambian communities.

Making energy access inclusive

Community energy initiatives have a long history of providing access to modern energy services in contexts where national governments are unable to provide infrastructure and commercial interests do not see profit. Examples thereof include the Cooperativa de Energia e Desenvolvimento Rural do Medio Uruguai Ltda (CRELUZ) in the Brazilian state of Rio Grande do Sul. CRELUZ was set up in the 1960s to improve the local supply of electricity. Initially, the co-operative managed local grid infrastructure and bought electricity from a national supplier in bulk which reduced the overall cost to end users. It was able to connect previously neglected households and eventually started to generate electricity from mini-hydro projects to provide more reliable supply (Ashden 2010a, 2010b).

The United States overcame the urban–rural divide of access to electricity through a co-operative model supported by President Roosevelt.

> Within four years following the close of the World War II, the number of rural electric systems in operation doubled, the number of consumers connected more than tripled and the miles of energized line grew more than five-fold. By 1953, more than 90 percent of U.S. farms had electricity.
>
> (NRECA, 2019a)

Today energy co-operatives in the US are estimated to serve 42 million people across forty-seven states (NRECA, 2019b).[9]

In decentralised community ownership structures, energy citizens are seen as key actors to "democratise the energy market" (Vansintjan, 2015, p. 7). However, Lennon et al. (2019) warn that the citizenship construct has its origins in the division between public and private spheres where women were traditionally excluded from decision making outside domestic settings and therefore from 'citizenship' altogether. Even today, there is recognition of limited diversity in the governing bodies of European community energy groups where men of a certain age and socio-economic background tend to dominate decision making (Van Veelen, 2018). In fact, a recent study looking at industrialised, emerging and developing energy economies shows that women are hugely underrepresented in technical and decision-making roles in the conventional energy sector. It argues that targeted actions and policies are required to provide opportunities for women in renewable energy transitions (Baruah, 2017). Similarly, Pearl-Martinez and Stephens (2016) conclude that "enhanced gender diversity among those involved in shaping energy systems will accelerate both social and technical change in the energy-system transition." In other words, greater gender equality in developing energy access is fundamental to delivering modern and renewable energy services for *all*.

The previous chapter established that traditional daily life and energy use in Kartong is gendered similarly to past divisions of labour in many industrialised countries. Women are responsible for the domestic sphere including household chores and caring for children (Greene, 2017). Without considering women's voices in decision making which affects energy consumption at household level, domestic renewable energy initiatives "risk being inappropriate and failing" (Abdullahi, 2017). Worse, they can "result in reverse outcomes of pro-environmental policy for the poor as well as for society in general" (Fakier, 2018, p. 166). The socio-cultural contexts which shape women's participation in renewable energy transitions and regarding the delivery of energy access therefore need to be understood and considered (Ferroukhi et al., 2019).

We have already seen that in the past women have not adopted the use of bicycles for localised transport or learnt to drive motorised vehicles linking Kartong with other settlements in the country. The often top-down and techno-centric decision-making processes risk overlooking the lived realities of local people, especially women. They can therefore also overstate the potential for leapfrogging (Murphy, 2001). Socio-cultural understanding of leapfrogging therefore has to suggest that women's participation in technical and decision-making processes regarding increased energy access is required. We need to ensure that energy citizenship in developing world contexts does not become another form of participatory 'tyranny' in which participation is forced on communities or segments of society are disempowered in the process (Cooke and Kothari, 2001).

The importance of gender equality is increasingly recognised in ECOWAS, which validated a regional policy on 'Gender mainstreaming in energy access' (Sow, 2015; AfDB, n.d.). Gender mainstreaming describes a policy approach to improve gender equality by taking into account both men's and women's aspirations, here in relation to improving access to modern energy. For The Gambia, a number of challenges and barriers in relation to women's participation have been highlighted, including "cultural norms and traditional practices" on the one hand and lack of advocacy at higher level decision making on the other (Ceesay and Gassama, n.d.). The issue of gender equality demonstrates the crucial link between understanding energy practices from the perspective of less powerful stakeholders and translating that insight into inclusive policy and practice.

The myth of leapfrogging

In Kartong, energy access was historically based on localised resources as part of sharing practices which provided essential access to food and mobility in energy-scarce households. However, as highlighted earlier, access to modern energy for lighting, communication or motorised transport was not delivered through a process of leapfrogging technologies. Instead there was a gradual adaptation in energy practices, as technologies or infrastructure became available over time, including ICTs and transport infrastructure.

Successful adaptation of modern energy systems and leapfrogging require advanced technical capabilities at household, community and national level. It is difficult to leapfrog to electric modes of transport if electricity infrastructure and generating capacity is insufficient. This also further highlights the entanglement of different energy technologies and practices and the need for more holistic understanding of the local energy metabolism.

Furthermore, leapfrogging should not merely be considered as a technological process but one that also considers socio-cultural practices, barriers and opportunities such as ownership and decision-making structures to ensure equitable access. Gender mainstreaming policies are therefore required in this context where energy practices have historically been gendered and decision making is orientated towards older men. In the past, gradual shifts in transport infrastructure have, for example, further cemented gender differences with men more likely to adopt new technologies and develop necessary skills such as riding bicycles or learning to drive a car.

Going forward, is Kartong any closer to access to modern energy for all? Has the community leapfrogged to renewable electricity? What factors shape Kartong's energy metabolism today? What are the trends and changes emerging in terms of everyday energy practices such as lighting, cooking and communication? And is the community overall moving towards modern energy based on sustainable and equitable energy access?

Notes

1 It is important to differentiate 'clean' – as in cooking fuels which do not significantly contribute to indoor air pollution – from other forms of 'clean' energy associated with debates surrounding power production. While some NGOs may use the term to describe renewable energy sources in industrialised contexts, it is also employed to greenwash polluting industries. Simms et al. (2010, pp. 83–84), for example, question the label of 'clean coal' that is used when discussing the potential extraction of greenhouse gases from coal based electricity generation: "Despite the environmental burden from the mining of coal, stick the word clean in front of it, and suddenly it becomes palatable." Also see the section on 'food practices' in Chapter 4.
2 The recent collapse of travel operator Thomas Cook, responsible for an estimated 40% of tourists in The Gambia, is likely to have a negative impact on the country's tourism industry (Saine, 2019).
3 Participant 15, interviewed by author, Berending, 15 August 2010.
4 Rather than being associated with product semantics of technical equipment such as charge controllers, the traffic light on Kairaba Avenue is an important landmark that serves as reference point when giving directions. Today it even shows up on Google Maps when searching for 'The Gambia traffic light.'
5 The term community can refer to geographically defined communities, communities of interest or combinations of both.

6 This definition is based on consensus derived between the twelve partners of the Community Power (www.communitypower.eu) project, and at times opposing insights of different European contexts. The word co-operative for instance was deemed as capitalist by some Scottish stakeholders whereas it had communist connotations in former Soviet countries.

7 'Shares' in energy co-operatives are unlike those found on the stock exchange. They are non-tradable and their value does not fluctuate. For more information, Sharenergy, an organisation that supports communities to set up energy co-operative in the UK, provides a concise overview on its website (www.sharenergy.coop/investing).

8 The national grid in The Gambia is currently comprised of several smaller grids as opposed to one large interconnected network.

9 The co-operatives manage grid infrastructure, that does not mean that electricity flowing through is generated from renewable sources.

References

Abdullahi, A.A. (2017) An analysis of the role of women in curbing energy poverty in Nigeria. *Journal of Sustainable Development Studies*, 10 (2), pp. 45–60.

Adhekpukoli, E. (2018) The democratization of electricity in Nigeria. *The Electricity Journal*, 31, pp. 1–6. https://doi.org/10.1016/j.tej.2018.02.007

AfDB (n.d.) *Draft: ECOWAS policy for gender mainstreaming in energy access*. Abidjan: African Development Bank. Available from: <www.afdb.org/fileadmin/uploads/afdb/Documents/Generic-Documents/ECOWAS_Policy_for_Gender_Mainstreaming_in_Energy_Access.pdf> [Accessed 27 November 2019].

Alzouma, G. (2005) Myths of digital technology in Africa leapfrogging development? *Global Media and Communication*, 1 (3), pp. 339–356. https://doi.org/10.1177/1742766505058128

APP (2015) *Africa progress report: Seizing Africa's energy and climate opportunities*. Geneva: Africa Progress Panel.

Ashden (2010a) *CRELUZ, Brazil, hydro-power for the community: Ashden award winner* [Online video], 7 July. Available from: <www.youtube.com/watch?v=BSWaqN0IoXk> [Accessed 21 October 2019].

Ashden (2010b) *Cooperativa de Energia e Desenvolvimento Rural do Médio Uruguai Ltda. (CRELUZ) / Micro-hydro makes the grid reliable* [Online]. Available from: <www.ashden.org/winners/cooperativa-de-energia-e-desenvolvimento-rural-do-m%C3%A9dio-uruguai-ltda-creluz> [Accessed 21 October 2019].

Assefa, G. (2011) *Leapfrogging possibilities for sustainable consumption and production in Africa: An overview*. Bonn: Federal Ministry for the Environment, Nature Conservation and Nuclear Safety.

Baruah, B. (2017) Renewable inequity? Women's employment in clean energy in industrialized, emerging and developing economies. *Natural Resources Forum*. https://doi.org/10.1111/1477-8947.12105

Batinge, B., Musango, J.K. and Brent, A.C. (2019) Sustainable energy transition framework for unmet electricity markets. *Energy Policy*, 129, pp. 1090–1099. https://doi.org/10.1016/j.enpol.2019.03.016

Bazilian, M., Welsch, M., Divan, D., Elzinga, D., Strbac, G., Howells, M., Jones, L., Keane, A., Gielen, D., Balijepalli, V.S.K.M., Brew-Hammond, A. and Yumkella,

K. (2011) *Smart and just grids: Opportunties for sub-Saharan Africa*. London: Imperial College London.

Bhattacharyya, S.C. (2012) Energy access programmes and sustainable development: A critical review and analysis. *Energy for Sustainable Development*, 16 (3), pp. 260–271. https://doi.org/10.1016/j.esd.2012.05.002

Boko, G.M.J. (2003) Air pollution and respiratory diseases in African big cities: The case of cotonou in Benin. In: Bunch, M.J., Suresh, V.M. and Kumaran, T.V. eds. *Proceedings of the third international conference on environment and health, December 15–17, 2003, Chennai*. Chennai: Department of Geography, University of Madras and Faculty of Environmental Studies, York University, pp. 32–43.

Burke, M.J. and Stephens, J.C. (2017) Energy democracy: Goals and policy instruments for sociotechnical transitions. *Energy Research & Social Science*, 33, pp. 35–48.

Ceesay, K.K. and Gassama, A. (n.d.) Status of gender mainstreaming in energy access in the Gambia [Online presentation]. In: *Regional Validation Workshop for the ECOWAS Policy for Gender Mainstreaming in Energy Access*. Praia: ECOWAS Centre for Renewable Energy and Energy Efficiency.

Cooke, B. and Kothari, U., eds. (2001) *Participation: The new tyranny?* London/ New York: Zed Books.

Dakar Challenge (n.d.) *About us*. Available from: <www.dakarchallenge.co.uk/about-us/> [Accessed 16 October 2019].

Davison, R., Vogel, D., Harris, D. and Jones, N. (2000) Leapfrogging in developing countries: An inevitable luxury? *The Electronic Journal of Information Systems in Developing Countries*, 1 (5), pp. 1–10.

Diop, D., Zwanenburg, M. and Pasdeloup, M.V. (2014) *The Gambia SE4ALL: Action agenda*. Freiburg: Particip GmbH.

Edwards, S. (2017) Developed countries "exporting pollution" by trading second-hand vehicles to poorer countries, experts say. *Devex* [Online], 26 January. Available from: <www.devex.com/news/developed-countries-exporting-pollution-by-trading-second-hand-vehicles-to-poorer-countries-experts-say-89457> [Accessed 5 April 2019].

Espinosa, P. (2018) Technological innovation key to Paris goals. *UN Climate Speech*, 26 November. Available from: <https://unfccc.int/news/espinosa-technological-innovation-key-to-paris-goals> [Accessed 3 April 2019].

Essoh, N.P.S. (2013) Shipping and invasion of second-hand vehicles in West African ports: Analysing the factors and market effects at the port of Abidjan. *American Journal of Industrial and Business Management*, 3, pp. 209–221. http://dx.doi.org/10.4236/ajibm.2013.32026

Ezeoha, A., Okoyeuzu, C., Onah, E. and Uche, C. (2019) Second-hand vehicle markets in West Africa: A source of regional disintegration, trade informality and welfare losses. *Business History*, 61 (1: Changing Secondhand Economies), pp. 187–204. https://doi.org/10.1080/00076791.2018.1459087

Fakier, K. (2018) Women and renewable energy in a South African community: Exploring energy poverty and environmental racism. *Journal of International Women's Studies*, 19 (5), pp. 165–176.

Ferroukhi, R., Renner, M., Nagpal, D., García-Baños, C. and Barua, B. (2019) *Renewable energy: A gender perspective*. Abu Dhabi: International Renewable Energy Agency.

Goldemberg, J. (1998) Leapfrog energy technologies. *Energy Policy*, 26 (10), pp. 729–741.

Greene, M. (2017) Paths, projects and careers of domestic practice: Exploring dynamics of demand over biographical time. In: Hui, A., Day, R. and Walker, G. eds. (2018) *Demanding energy: Space, time and change*. Hampshire: Palgrave Macmillan Publishers Ltd.

Harvey, F. (2015) Developing countries could leapfrog west with clean energy, says Hollande. *The Guardian* [Online], 3 June. Available from: <www.theguardian.com/environment/2015/jun/03/developing-countries-could-leapfrog-west-with-clean-energy-says-hollande> [Accessed 9 December 2018].

IEA (2017) *WEO energy access Outlook 2017: Methodology for energy access analysis*. Paris: IEA Publications.

James, J. (2014) Relative and absolute components of leapfrogging in mobile phones by developing countries. *Telematics and Informatics*, 31, pp. 52–61. https://doi.org/10.1016/j.tele.2013.03.001

Jarju, M. (2019) Gambia: President Barrow Lays foundation stone for OMVG substation. *Foroyaa/All Africa* [Online], 25 February. Available from: <https://allafrica.com/stories/201902260296.html> [Accessed 21 October 2019].

Kumar, R.V. (2015) Leapfrogging to sustainable power. In: Heap, B. ed. *Smart villages: New thinking for off-grid communities worldwide*. Cambridge: University of Cambridge, pp. 35–41.

Lennon, B., Dunphy, N., Gaffney, C., Revez, A, Mullally, G. and O'Connor, P. (2019) Citizen or consumer? Reconsidering energy citizenship. *Journal of Environmental Policy & Planning*. https://doi.org/10.1080/1523908X.2019.168027

Makonese, T., Ifegbesan, A.P. and Rampedi, I.T. (2018) Household cooking fuel use patterns and determinants across southern Africa: Evidence from the demographic and health survey data. *Energy & Environment*, 29 (1), pp. 29–48. https://doi.org/10.1177/0958305X17739475

Manneh, M. (2013) *Wind energy projects grid-connected case study in the Gambia* [Online presentation]. Praia: Ministry of Energy (The Gambia). Available from: <www.ecreee.org/sites/default/files/event-att/presentation_on_wind_energy_in_the_gambia_manneh_ecreee_energy_workshop.pdf> [Accessed 20 October 2019].

Marriott, J. and Minio-Paluello, M. (2012) *The oil road: Journeys from the Caspian Sea to the city of London*. London: Verso.

Mitchell, J. and Faal, J. (2006) *The Gambian tourist value chain and prospects for pro-poor tourism* [Draft report]. London: Overseas Development Institute.

Murphy, J.T. (2001) Making the energy transition in rural East Africa: Is leapfrogging an alternative? *Technological Forecasting & Social Change*, 68, pp. 173–193.

NRECA (2019a) *America's electric cooperatives: 2017 fact sheet* [Online]. Arlington: National Rural Electric Cooperative Association. Available from: <www.electric.coop/electric-cooperative-fact-sheet/> [Accessed 18 October 2019].

NRECA (2019b) *History: The history behind America's electric co-operatives and NRECA* [Online]. Arlington: National Rural Electric Cooperative Association. Available from: <www.electric.coop/our-organization/history/> [Accessed 18 October 2019].

Pachauri, S., Rao, N.D., Nagai, Y. and Riahi, K. (2012) *Access to modern energy: Assessment and Outlook for developing and emerging regions*. Laxenburg: International Institute for Applied Systems Analysis.

Pearl-Martinez, R. and Stephens, J.C. (2016) Toward a gender diverse workforce in the renewable energy transition. *Sustainability: Science, Practice and Policy*, 12 (1), pp. 8–15. https://doi.org/10.1080/15487733.2016.11908149

PURA (n.d.) *Approval of tariffs* [Online]. Serrekunda: Public Utilities Regulatory Authority. Available from: <www.pura.gm/tariffs/> [Accessed 16 October 2019].

Raja, S. and Christiaensen, L. (2017) *The future of work requires more, not less technology in developing countries*. Jobs Notes, (2). Hamburg: Jobs Group, World Bank Group.

Roberts, J., Bodman, F. and Rybski, R. (2014) *Community power: Model legal frameworks for citizen-owned renewable energy*. London: ClientEarth.

Saine, P. (2019) Gambia fears tourism crisis after Thomas Cook collapse. *Reuters*, 26 September. Available from: <https://uk.reuters.com/article/us-thomas-cook-grp-investment-gambia/gambia-fears-tourism-crisis-after-thomas-cook-collapse-idUKKBN1WB1UT> [Accessed 21 October 2019].

Sambodo, M.T. and Novandra, R. (2019) The state of energy poverty in Indonesia and its impact on welfare. *Energy Policy*, 132, pp. 113–121. https://doi.org/10.1016/j.enpol.2019.05.029

Sarabhai, K. and Vyas, P. (2017) The leapfrogging opportunity: The role of education in sustainable development and climate change mitigation. *European Journal of Education*, 52 (4), pp. 427–436. https://doi.org/10.1111/ejed.12243

Schiffer, A. (2014) *From remote island grids to urban solar co-operatives*. Edinburgh: Friends of the Earth Scotland.

Shoichet, C.E., Griffiths, J. and Flournoy, D. (2016) Berta Cáceres, Honduran activist, killed. *CNN* [Online], 4 March. Available from: <https://edition.cnn.com/2016/03/03/americas/honduras-activist-berta-caceres-killed/index.html> [Accessed 22 March 2019].

Simms, A., Johnson, V. and Chowla, P. (2010) *Growth isn't possible: Why we need a new economic direction*. London: New Economics Foundation.

Singh, G., Nouhou, S.A. and Sokona, M.Y. (2013) *The Gambia: Renewables readiness assessment 2013*. Abu Dhabi: IRENA.

Sow, F.T. (2015) *ECOWAS regional validation workshop for the ECOWAS policy for gender mainstreaming in energy access*. Dakar: Economic Community of West African States.

Starkey, P. and Hine, J. (2014) *Poverty and sustainable transport: How transport affects poor people with policy implications for poverty reduction*. London: ODI.

Steinmueller, W.E. (2008) ICTs and the possibility for leapfrogging by developing countries. *International Labour Review*, 140 (2), pp. 193–210. DOI: 10.1111/j.1564-913x.2001.tb00220.x

Vansintjan, D. (2015) The energy transition to energy democracy: Power to the people: Final results oriented report of the REScoop 20–20–20 Intelligent Energy Europe project. REScoop 20–20–20.

Van Veelen, B. (2018) Negotiating energy democracy in practice: Governance processes in community energy projects. *Environmental Politics*, 27 (4), pp. 644–665. DOI: 10.1080/09644016.2018.1427824

Wu, J. and Wu, T. (2015) Goal 7: Ensure access to affordable, reliable, sustainable and modern energy for all. *UN Chronicle*, 51 (4). Available from: <https://unchronicle.un.org/article/goal-7-ensure-access-affordable-reliable-sustainable-and-modern-energy-all> [Accessed 16 October 2019].

You, K., Dal Bianco, S., Lin, Z. and Amankwah-Amoah, J. (2019) Bridging technology divide to improve business environment: Insights from African nations. *Journal of Business Research*, 97, pp. 268–280. https://doi.org/10.1016/j.jbusres.2018.01.015

4 Current energy practices
Everyday life in a local compound

Building on themes previously established, this chapter explores everyday energy practices in present day Kartong. These are firstly described through two narrative texts which are based on regular immersions in the compound of the Sambou family. They enabled me to observe and participate in everyday family life and by extension the wider community. An earlier version of 'A day in the life of Sambou Kunda' was published in 2016 as part of an article for the *Energy Research and Social Science* journal under the title 'Empowered, excited, or disenfranchised? Unveiling issues of energy access inequality and resource dependency in The Gambia.' The sections, 'A day in Sambou Kunda' and 'A day in the rainy season' present first updates based on two visits at the beginning of 2018 and an immersion in July 2019. This is followed by a situated analysis of how technological changes intersect with changes in energy practices and growing demand for modern energy.

A day in Sambou Kunda

The temperature has cooled down overnight and the air is hazy due to strong Harmattan winds that carry a lot of dust in the air. Traffic on the tarred Kombo Coastal Road which runs past Sambou Kunda is picking up as the morning progresses. Women are balancing baskets on their heads on the way to the market or pushing wheelbarrows with goods. Others are carrying empty buckets and tools to their vegetable gardens. Boys are cycling past with cardboard boxes full of fresh bread, which are distributed from several local bakeries to shops and roadside stalls across Kartong. Sometimes they are delivered to neighbouring villages if there is demand and vice versa.

The bicycle repair shop across the road is receiving its first customers (Figure 4.1). With the predominately sandy roads punctures are commonplace. A shopkeeper passes in front with a wheelbarrow full of rubbish on his way to one of the local dumps and again on his way back.[1] Shortly after,

Figure 4.1 Bicycle repair shop

a number of bicycle traders pass by carrying radios or pots. Earlier this morning, they crossed the river from Casamance buying and selling goods on their journey. Traveling in the opposite direction, a group of children are walking to school, which is located past the market towards the end of the settlement area. They will soon be joined by pupils from the neighbouring village of Berending who park their bicycles outside the repair shop. A charity donated the bicycles so that both boys and girls could easily get to school.

Adding to all this hustle and bustle are roaming goats and sheep along with playing children and various types of motorised vehicles. Suddenly, four cars carrying Western tourists speed through the village beeping loudly for pedestrians to get out of the way. They may have arrived on one of the few planes that can occasionally be seen flying in the skies above Kartong and stay in one of the tourist lodges along the southern coast of The Gambia. Locals from Kartong and neighbouring villages often find employment there.

While the traffic passes outside, friends and extended family members drop into Sambou Kunda to greet and see how everyone is. This is an important ritual that signifies the continued strong social ties within the community. The oldest of six Sambou brothers pulls out a large sitting mat and spreads it on the veranda that connects several of the Sambou Kunda households which are located around an inner courtyard. He fetches his ataya set, including charcoal, a small metal burner, tea and sugar. He used to listen to the news on his battery powered radio but when it broke it could not be fixed to produce the same quality of sound and so he gave it away. Several men have dropped by to join him for ataya and to chat. They are occasionally interrupted by a ringing phone or a young child carrying a message. Some of the men will stay for breakfast, others will come back after lunch, when it is the younger brother's turn to brew for them (Figure 4.2).

In the meantime, the older brother's wife has returned from watering her garden and is now setting up her stall on the roadside to sell bread with homemade *njebe*, a spicy bean filling. She provides a popular breakfast alternative to what is available from local shops which commonly sell bread with chocolate or egg mayonnaise. A number of local bakeries produce baguette-like *tapalapa* in large wood-fired ovens, but over the past few years have also been producing a softer alternative called *senfu*. A boy on his bike drops off *senfu* directly to the wife's stall on his distribution round. Breakfast foods tend to be accompanied by hot tea or instant coffee which she also sells.

Inside, the younger brother's wife uses an electric kettle which she shares with other women in the compound to heat water for breakfast. Throughout the day, the kettle can be seen moving between different Sambou Kunda households, to heat water for beverages or bucket showers. Until recently the wife relied on bottled gas to quickly boil water for hot drinks in the morning but the kettle provides a more convenient alternative. She also uses it to heat water for producing larger quantities of juices made from various local ingredients including the fruit of the baobab tree, ginger or *wonjo*, which is made

Figure 4.2 Men chatting and brewing ataya

Figure 4.3 Producing wonjo juice

from hibiscus leaves (Figure 4.3). She procured a fridge around the time her household was connected to the grid nearly five years ago. Ever since she has been using it to chill her homemade drinks which she sells either in small quantities wrapped up in plastic bags or in re-used plastic bottles to customers who often come by the house.[2] Using the fridge for business purposes takes priority over preserving food for the household. Fresh produce for cooking is still bought from the market (Figure 4.4), while some foods are preserved by drying them out in the sun (Figure 4.5). Only fresh fish is commonly put in fridges which are shared with neighbours, friends or family who do not own a fridge themselves. In contrast, large quantities of fish are smoked in houses on the river and beach sides (Figure 4.6).[3]

As the day continues three boys accompany a donkey cart filled with firewood on the road, and a man passes with firewood on the back of his bike. Firewood is still the most common cooking fuel in Kartong. In larger family compounds like Sambou Kunda, wives, daughters and co-wives take it in turn to cook lunch for extended family members. Several of the Sambou women have gone to the market to pick up ingredients or sent children to run errands in preparation for lunch. The thumping of large wooden mortar and pestles can be heard in many parts of the village. While this is traditionally

Figure 4.4 Kartong market

Figure 4.5 Drying grains in the sun

Figure 4.6 Inside of river side fish smoking house

used to grind up ingredients to prepare sauces, women nowadays also pay to have rice husks removed by a noisy diesel-powered machine instead of pounding it. Several of the machines are located in different parts of the community but only one is currently working.

In Sambou Kunda, a large kitchen building serves one part of the compound for communal cooking. Until recently the space would fill up with smoke as meals were prepared over the traditional three stones on the floor with burning firewood in between and a cooking pot balanced on top (Figure 4.7). The kitchen has received an upgrade and cooking now takes place over a raised platform enabling women to stand up but there has only been a minimal reduction in smoke as the platform is located next to some pre-existing ventilation holes (Figure 4.8).

Lunch time is approaching and the call for prayer sounds from several local mosques. Shops along the main road close up as people perform ablutions[4] and pray before they break for lunch. Some will open in the afternoon, others in the evening. In Sambou Kunda people huddle around large bowls set out on the veranda or the courtyard to eat communally. Men usually eat in one group. Women form another group and can be seen training meal etiquette to their children which includes carefully scooping rice from the side of the bowl closest to oneself using the right hand or a spoon. Anyone passing is told *na domo* – come eat. Lunch is comprised of a rice dish topped with a

Figure 4.7 Kitchen outhouse (April 2011)

Figure 4.8 Upgraded kitchen (January 2018)

sauce cooked with vegetables and accompanied by local fish or occasionally chicken. Goat, sheep or cow meat is only served at special occasions such as naming ceremonies or religious celebrations. At the time of Ramadan the otherwise daily cycle of food preparation drastically changes. During the annual forty-day period when Muslims fast, meals are taken after the sun has set which leads to women cooking at night whilst otherwise continuing with normal chores during the day.

Outside after lunch, traffic picks up again. Men gather and sit along the road to talk and drink ataya. A group of younger men is chatting under a mango tree nearby, when one of them gets up to offer an elderly woman who is walking to the far end of the settlement area a lift in his car. He will be back shortly to continue the discussion with his peers.

In the meantime, women or children wash basins with water from a tap in the courtyard that is intermittently fed from a central borehole which serves the community through a network of public pipes and increasing numbers of private taps (Figure 4.9). Centrally, water is pumped with power from solar panels that were upgraded just a few years ago (see 'Sufficiency as a behavioural approach' section in Chapter 5). However, the system struggles to meet the ever-growing demand, exacerbated by a lack of sunshine during Harmattan that covers the solar panels in dust. Women fill up containers when the taps are working and store water until it is needed. In addition, they draw water from an old household well located at the back

Figure 4.9 Water tank with new solar panels (2014)

of the compound. It provides a reliable source when the taps are closed, is conveniently located for hand washing clothes,[5] but requires more physical effort (Figure 4.10).

Some of the Sambou Kunda women make their way back to their vegetable gardens to water more crops using shallow wells dug into the sand. Gardens are fenced with branch-like growths from the top of palm trees locally known as *pamparan*. During the dry season, it is important to protect crops from cows that tend to roam freely. Pamaparan is relatively cheap but only lasts two to three years and there are plenty of tales amongst vegetable gardeners where cows have destroyed entire crops in an instant. Some of the vegetables such as onions and tomatoes will be used at home, some sold at the local market and others are destined for Brikama and Serrekunda or bought there and sold in Kartong (Figure 4.11).

While many women grow vegetables, men tend to focus more on cash crops such as fruit orchards. An elder in Sambou Kunda grows mangos while one of the Sambou brothers started cultivating an orange orchard a few years ago with nursery trees imported from Casamance. He initially used barbed wire fencing to protect the young trees from roaming cows but to no avail. Then a friend shot a vulture for him and suggested to keep it rotting in a bucket with water. Sprinkling the liquid onto the young trees was more effective than the fence and he used the method until the trees were established and no longer in danger.

As the evening approaches, women return from their fields. A boy is pushing a wheelbarrow filled with firewood past Sambou Kunda while another carries a pile on the back of his bicycle. The wind picks up as the sun sets and the first electric bulbs located along exterior walls of buildings on the Kombo Coastal Road turn on. The call for prayer erupts and the bike repair shop closes for the day. Other shops shut briefly to perform religious duties but will open again once these are completed.

Motorised traffic has slowed down and eventually a bus that left early in the morning for Banjul returns to Kartong. Along the road towards Gunjur, about a kilometre north of the main settlement area, cow herders have lit a large wood fire to keep young calves warm during the night. Similarly, some families in the less densely populated part of Kartong have lit fires. Though the temperature in The Gambia hardly drops below 16 degrees Celsius, locals walking up and down the street past Sambou Kunda are wearing woolly hats and winter coats, feeling the cold coming from the sea. They say Kartong has a microclimate that makes it cooler than other parts of the country. Apart from the occasional motorcycle or car, a bush taxi belonging to a Kartonka continues to operate until around midnight. Across the road a sewing machine can be heard running late into the night as a tailor is working under a single naked lightbulb. In contrast, a tailor who stays

Figure 4.10 Washing clothes with compound well in the background

Figure 4.11 Vegetable gardener amongst her onion crop protected by pamapran fencing

Figure 4.12 Exterior lights illuminate the road before the sun comes up

in Sambou Kunda has decided to finish working and come into one of the houses to watch television.

At nighttime, the road outside is quiet except for the occasional goat, pig and donkey wandering past or through Sambou Kunda, causing a racket as they look for food. Dogs can be heard barking and cats trample across the corrugated roofs of houses fighting with each other. As dawn approaches the first lights are turned on and two fishermen who rent a room in Sambou Kunda get ready to leave for work. Shortly after, the oldest of the Sambou brothers appears, waiting for the bus that travels to Banjul. It leaves from the market, then stops to pick up more people outside the mosque before continuing on its journey. Cockerels are crowing, the call for prayer sounds nearby and people start walking towards the mosque guided by lights on exterior walls along the road (Figure 4.12). Men on bikes pass holding mobile phone torches as they cycle and overtake the Sambou Kunda elder and his wife. A new day begins.

Life during the rainy season

It is now 14 months later and the beginning of the rainy season. Women across Kartong have abandoned their vegetable gardens until the next growing season and families should have started preparing their rice fields. However, the rain has yet to start and there have only been a few brief showers over the past weeks. Earlier this year a bush fire destroyed large areas of the forest towards Berending including parts of the orange orchard belonging to one of the Sambou brothers. Small forest fires will continue to threaten people's land until the rain arrives.

The weather is hot and humid and in one of the Sambou Kunda households, several standing fans have been running all night to keep people cool while they sleep. A ceiling fan was recently mounted in the main living space to reduce the heat during the day or when people watch television. Immediately next to it, a naked energy-efficient lightbulb illuminates the otherwise dark room which sees limited natural daylight. Similarly, a lightbulb in the corridor that connects the living space with several bedrooms and an outside bathroom tends to be on continuously throughout day and night.

Sweeping brushes can be heard across the compound as women and girls prepare for the day. A water tap is running, filling up containers in the outside bathroom that will later be used for bucket showers, cooking, cleaning basins, floors and washing clothes. There is also a new washing machine in the bathroom which the wife prefers to use since she fell in the house carrying a large bucket of water and injured her hip. However, something causes the machine to stop abruptly, requiring her to frequently press the start button and she struggles with the instructions which are in Dutch. For now, she uses both traditional hand washing and modern practices. Wet clothes quickly dry outside in the sun before they are pressed using an electric iron that is shared between several households in the compound and which has replaced charcoal predecessors used until recently.

Outside, the traffic picks up throughout the morning with passing taxis, motorcycles and people walking or cycling. Not long ago some local youths took it upon themselves to install a 'sleeping policeman' in the form of painted tyres and tree trunks placed on the road during daylight hours to help slow down traffic (Figure 4.13). The other day, however, the actual police were called and asked for the contraption to be removed, perhaps after one of the taxi drivers made a complaint about the obstacle slowing him down. Right next to it, a man has established a 'car wash,' turning the increased traffic into a business opportunity. He operates an industrial vacuum cleaner with a long extension lead connected to electricity at a nearby compound.

As people are moving up and down the street, some stop on the Sambou Kunda shop front where a young Sambou wife has established a second stall to prepare breakfast and sell hot drinks. She has to run back and forth to fill up a flask with water boiled by a kettle. Inside the compound, the wife

Figure 4.13 Temporary installation of 'sleeping policeman'

who previously shared a kettle with other women to prepare breakfast or to heat water for bucket showers has gone back to using a gas burner because her kettle broke down. When she prepares meals for extended family members in the shared kitchen on one side of the compound she continues to rely on firewood. The space has received another upgrade (Figure 4.14) and now includes a chimney, which has drastically improved the indoor air quality when preparing meals. This is in contrast to kitchens on the other side of the compound that continue to fill up with smoke while women cook.

Last week there were several celebrations including a large naming ceremony that took place in nearby Tourey Kunda. Women from Sambou Kunda went to help prepare food. The following day women from across the community joined those in Sambou Kunda as the compound hosted a traditional Koranic reading. Around 150–200 people converged with men gathering in the courtyard while the women met in another part of the compound to jointly prepare traditional foods in a maze of extra-large pots cooking over wooden fires (Figure 4.15).

Since the festivities, boys and men have been gathering regularly in one of the Sambou Kunda households to watch the Africa Cup of Nations as it is being televised. In Sambou Kunda, electricity continues to be used for

Figure 4.14 Kitchen upgrade with chimney (July 2019)

Figure 4.15 Communal cooking during celebration

household chores, pleasure and business purposes. The tailor who is based in Sambou Kunda, for example, operates lights and an electric sewing machine. He also plays music until late into the night. The wife who produced home-made drinks a year ago has bought a second fridge to increase her production volume and moved the appliances into an empty storeroom on the shop front. However, one of the fridges is currently under repair.

There have been several small electricity extensions in Kartong that have increased grid coverage in a few places, including where two Sambou brothers have built a new compound. Accordingly, one of them has just procured a new fridge. However, large parts of the settlement remain unconnected (Figure 4.16). There has been a recent flurry of small solar installations but many households living on the edge of the grid complain of 'spoiled batteries' and instead rely on family and friendship networks to access electricity and charge mobile phones.

In contrast, all households in Sambou Kunda are electrified, either in small clusters or through individual meters. However, supply is frequently interrupted due to load shedding – rolling blackouts between different parts of the electricity grid. All of a sudden, the noise level drops as fans, televisions and music switch off. When this happens after dark people revert to candles, battery powered torches and mobile phone lights. Other times, households run out of money to top up the pay-as-you-go system,

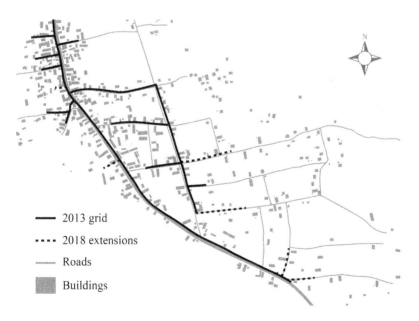

Figure 4.16 Detail of Kartong electricity grid

locally known as 'cash power.' Appliances switch off until more credit is purchased which can be done over the phone, from local vendors or directly from NAWEC outlets in Gunjur or Brikama. The latter offers the best rates but having to travel to these towns might not be economical or convenient.

In the evening, fishermen are returning home. A recently established Chinese-owned fishmeal factory has brought with it in an increase in migrant workers from Senegal and other parts of West Africa. A group of men are renting rooms in Sambou Kunda and pay one of the wives to cook for them. They struggle to access water for showers and ablutions when there is no pumped water available from the tap in the courtyard. Earlier this year, the central borehole that serves Kartong was disconnected from the solar panels and instead hooked up to a cash power meter to provide electricity for a new and more powerful pump.

The intention is to supply more energy to the borehole and so meet increasing demand. However, when there is no cash power or the Kartong grid is disconnected due to load shedding, this means there is also no running water. Due to the lack of rain and subsequently falling water table, the household well in Sambou Kunda has completely dried up. The workers have to walk to fetch what they need from one of the other neighbouring compounds where household wells still contain water. Otherwise, it is the women's role in Sambou Kunda to try and fill up buckets and containers to meet their family's demands throughout the day.

At night, the Sambou Kunda shop front along the Kombo Coastal Road is illuminated by electric lights. Motorised traffic is replaced by people walking and cycling up and down the street. Others gather in small groups in the courtyards of compounds or along the street to chat and brew ataya late into the night. There is a breeze coming from the nearby sea helping people, especially those without electric fans, to escape the heat that has stored up inside buildings during the day.

From low carbon mobility to car-centricity

The narratives above illustrate that for journeys within the settlement area walking and cycling continue to be the main forms of mobility. This includes attending the mosque, going to the market or visiting friends and family. However, it is evident that there is increasing reliance on motorised and fossil-fuel based transport, suggesting a further shift towards a linear energy metabolism. This is shaped by socio-political, socio-economic as well as spatial dimensions that relate to the expansion of the built environment and industrial developments.

Not long ago, motorised traffic was sparse, slow and largely confined to the tarred Kombo Coastal Road which in turn was dominated by Kartonkas walking and cycling. People from the urban areas would joke that one could sit in the middle of the road in Kartong and finish brewing ataya before another vehicle would pass. However, over the past few years, there has been a significant increase in motorcycles, privately owned cars, taxis and bush taxis (Figure 4.17) that can be seen traveling more and more on the sandy side streets to people's compounds or the border crossing east of Kartong.

＊ In a relatively short period, the Kombo Coastal Road that connects key social hubs including the main mosque, market and church, has been taken over by motorised vehicles throughout the day. Now cars can be observed aggressively beeping at pedestrians who have yet to adjust their behaviour and move out of the way of the new king in town. Irritated drivers treat the local road like they would traveling through other communities along main traffic arteries in The Gambia, unable to comprehend why it should be any different here.

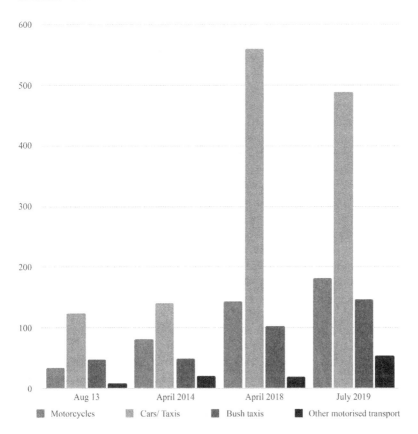

Figure 4.17 24h transport surveys show rise in motorised traffic

The potential hazards of speeding cars have not escaped the local residents' attention as illustrated by the installation of several signs urging drivers to slow down. As one commentator suggests: "we only hope the drivers respect them. [W]e should be looking forward to create humps if they fail to respect or obey the sign board."[6] The signs however have had little impact, not helped by the fact that the speedometer in many vehicles is broken, leading to the brief installation of the aforementioned 'sleeping policeman.'

Some locals suggest this increase in motorised traffic is due to the opening of the Chinese-owned fishmeal factory which is located on the Atlantic coast to the south of the settlement area. Large trucks servicing the site and increasing numbers of cars are now traveling through the village as opposed to stopping at the market to drop off and pick up passengers before turning around and traveling back north. There are parallels here to former sand mining in Kartong, which also contributed to heavy vehicle traffic. However, the entrance to the mining area was located towards the northern edge of the settlement and therefore had little impact on traffic flowing through the centre.[7] Other factors that may have contributed to the rise in traffic include the continuing expansion of the settlement area leading south in recent years.

The increase in taxis in particular provides a convenient service for those who do not have access to a private vehicle. Moreover, taxis also offer an important employment opportunity for young men in Kartong and beyond. This needs to be understood in the context of many deciding to travel the 'back way'[8] to Italy or other European countries 'looking for greener pastures' (Conrad Suso, 2019). There are countless stories of young Kartonkas who have embarked on the treacherous journey to enter Europe illegally. Not everybody has survived the journey unharmed. The driver of a bush taxi and his childhood friend who works as a taxi driver in Serrekunda embody this notion of motorised transport providing employment. This is in contrast to many of their peers who have tried to reach Europe, especially under the previous government regime. Whilst a more extensive bus service would reduce overall fossil fuel consumption it would also replace many of the jobs for male youth from Kartong and other villages and towns.

As it stands, there is a lack of alternative methods of motorised transport available. A limited bus service was introduced in 2013 and operates between Kartong and Banjul. However, it only leaves once a day early in the morning and returns late at night. It is a good option for some but does not meet the overall demand for travel. Unlike what elders recall about their experience growing up, these days people do not think about traveling to Banjul on foot. Few people cycle to neighbouring communities and even some of those involved in distributing bread locally now rely on motorcycles.

Whilst visiting the region during the 2019 rainy season, I also observed that bush taxis no longer wait to fill up with passengers on journeys between Kartong and Brikama. Previously, it was not uncommon for passengers to be sat waiting for an hour until a vehicle was full. However, the recent increase in motorised traffic and consequent competition between drivers means that passengers are no longer at the mercy of drivers but rather that drivers scramble for passengers and are willing to depart almost immediately. From the perspective of passengers this is much more convenient, especially as many journeys are indirect and require changing vehicles. Yet, the ever-increasing dependence on motorised transport goes hand in hand with dependence on imported, costly and polluting fossil fuels. This is further exacerbated by vehicles traveling at reduced passenger capacity leading to an overall increase in fossil fuel consumption, though it should be noted that some bush taxis have been replaced with smaller vehicles, compensating for the lower number of passengers per vehicle.

Divided electricity practices

For those who are grid connected, electricity is providing new services and economic opportunities. Fridges are used to cool drinks in Sambou Kunda which are sold and provide extra income for the women in the compound. Similarly, several tailoring businesses located along the Kombo Coastal Road can now decide if they want to pay for the maintenance of diesel generators to power larger sewing machines or simply use cash power.

However, since its arrival in Kartong, the coverage of the electricity grid has been limited to the older, more established parts of the settlement, leaving large areas unconnected. Resulting access inequality is therefore determined by the geographic location of households in relation to the grid.

The area not covered previously coincided with the part of Kartong that also lacked infrastructure to supply clean drinking water from the central borehole. The latter has since been provided. Nonetheless, households that were in close proximity to public water taps were also likely to be close to electricity lines when the grid first arrived. As such, grid access actually exacerbated local inequalities at the time (Wu et al., 2016, p. 35; Schiffer, 2016).

Today, the spatial divide of grid infrastructure becomes especially visible at night. Outside of Sambou Kunda, the Kombo Coastal Road is illuminated in places by electric lightbulbs people have placed along exterior walls of their compounds. The bulbs visualise who has cash power, whilst also providing informal street lighting that serves the wider community. In contrast, turning east and walking down the sandy roads past the edge of the electricity grid towards Balanta Kunda and beyond, the only light on the street when the moon is not visible is the occasional torch, mobile phone screen or glowing tip of a cigarette.

Depending on purchasing power and preference, candles and battery powered lights remain the main source of household lighting. Some also use contraptions known as *kura lampo* (electricity lamp). These consist of LEDs that are extracted from cheap torches fastened high up on ceilings or walls and are connected via cable to wooden boxes which house disposable batteries. Before the grid arrived, these were commonly used across Kartong. In addition, some compounds still burn large fires outside to provide lighting and for people to huddle round and keep warm during cooler parts of the year.

Adopting modern communication

Access to grid electricity has allowed televisions to become much more common and to play a significant role in present-day communication channels. Similar to the way exterior lightbulbs demonstrate which households have cash power, the increase in television usage at local level is made visible by the spread of ubiquitous satellite dishes that have been added to the landscape of Kartong in the past few years. Owning a television also has a certain status attached to it and it is better to have a broken set on display than not to own one at all. In a typical front room, which is preferably furnished with opulent-looking sofas and a coffee table, the television is added to the ornate display cabinet. Yet the novelty has also started to wear off. When households in Sambou Kunda first obtained television sets, these appeared to be constantly on even when no one was watching. Now they are mainly used at nighttime, yet conversations with people dropping by still take priority over watching movies.

Since the first mobile phones became available at the turn of the century, they have taken on an increasingly important communication role long before grid electricity reached Kartong. Initially, people charged their mobile phones at a number of different locations across the community where off-grid electricity was available, usually in exchange for a small fee. As one example, people would pay a small amount on top of the entrance fee to video clubs to have their phones charged whilst also watching a game of football. Likewise, one of two mobile phone receptor masts that serviced Kartong was previously located on the southern part of the settlement. It relied on a large off-grid diesel generator to power it and the security guard also used it to charge phones for those living nearby. Eventually the diesel generator and his job became obsolete when the mast was moved to a more central location and connected to the grid. The informal mobile phone charging sector virtually disappeared overnight when grid electricity arrived in Kartong. Despite the fact that only a small number of households were initially connected to the grid, people were able to charge phones at friends' and family members' compounds (Munro and Schiffer, 2019). However, mobile phone charging businesses have started to reappear in recent years to provide a service for the increasing numbers of migrant workers employed in the fishing industry.

Traditional brick phones that allow users to make phone calls and send text messages are still in use but are being replaced by smart phones. In turn, these provide additional functions such as access to social media and internet-based calls. Within the last decade a number of failed attempts to provide online services through a local internet cafe have been superseded by access through these personal devices. Even cash power can be topped up via mobile phone making it much more convenient compared with just a few years ago when people had no choice but to travel to Gunjur or Brikama to purchase additional credit (Munro and Schiffer, 2019). In turn, this demonstrates a kind of symbiosis between consuming electricity to power phones and using phones themselves to provide access to electricity at household level.

Changing household practices

Daily chores remain gendered with women largely responsible for fetching water, cooking and washing. In these roles, women have adapted electric gadgets such as irons and kettles which are typically shared between different households across a compound. Similarly, larger electrical equipment is shared between households as people leave fresh fish in others' fridges.

However, the transition to different technologies is not a linear process but adaptation is instead fluid: new equipment becomes available and replaces or is used in parallel with older technologies. When it breaks, people may revert back to previous practices (Pfeiffer and Mulder, 2013). In Sambou Kunda, one household recently reverted back to using a gas stove to heat water after an electric kettle broke. In comparison, a new washing machine continues to be used in parallel to traditional hand washing.

The fluidity of how and when technologies are adapted also depends on seasonal household requirements which result in changing energy practices over the course of a year. Fans for cooling, for example, are more commonly used during the hot and humid rainy season. Similarly, there are seasonal differences in relation to cooking practices (e.g. Ramadan) but overall change has been less drastic as locally sourced firewood is still the main cooking fuel and practices largely revolve around it. Boys continue to be responsible for fetching firewood while women take it in turn to cook for the wider family in larger communal kitchens. In Sambou Kunda, one of the kitchen outhouses has received several upgrades, but women are still exposed to smoke and pollution associated with burning biomass in other parts of the compound. Cooking practices can therefore not be described as clean. Only as women cook on gas, which they sometimes do when they are preparing meals for immediate family members, could it be argued that they are using a 'clean' fuel. This has to be understood with caution: regarding women's health, gas might be a preferred option as it reduces the significant health risks associated with indoor air pollution caused by burning biomass such as firewood or charcoal. However, bottled gas available in Kartong is an imported fossil fuel. In the context of energy access, it is therefore important to differentiate between 'clean' as in renewable cooking fuels and 'clean' in the sense that energy sources do not significantly contribute to indoor air pollution (Owili et al., 2017). Without biogas alternatives, cooking on natural or liquefied petroleum gas contributes to the overall shift towards dependence on imported and costly fossil fuels in Kartong and a linear energy metabolism to deliver modern energy services.

Towards a linear energy metabolism

In the transition to modern energy it is evident that Kartong has continued to move towards a linear energy metabolism. This is increasingly locking the community into fossil fuels for not just one but three key services: growing demand for motorised transport, electricity for households and businesses, and most recently also access to water from a central borehole which uses grid electricity to operate a pump.

Depending on household preferences and purchasing power, bottled gas which is used by some to prepare small meals or heat water contributes to this increasingly linear system, though firewood remains the main cooking fuel overall. Women are still responsible for cooking and therefore their respiratory health is more likely to be impacted by burning wood fuels, especially when cooking takes places in small semi-closed spaces. Although a few cooking facilities in Kartong may have been upgraded there is certainly no sign of leapfrogging to modern and clean cooking practices based on renewable energy.

Access to modern energy (and electricity in particular) is commonly associated with meeting wider development goals such as economic opportunities and access to healthcare (Schwerhoff and Sy, 2017; Adair-Rohani et al., 2013). Situated knowledge offered through the perspective of everyday practices surrounding Sambou Kunda provides a more integrated as well as nuanced understanding of energy practices in relation to modern energy available. For example, economic benefits associated are highly gendered.

The increase in fossil-fuelled transport provides a significant employment opportunity for young men who work as taxi drivers. In contrast, women are more likely to be engaged in operating juice-making businesses or breakfast stalls supported through access to electric fridges and kettles.

Furthermore, while there have been changes in communication, cooling and lighting practices for households that are grid connected, there is a strong spatial inequality between those who have cash power and those who have been geographically excluded. Thus far off-grid solar installations have not provided an adequate alternative for the majority of Kartonkas living beyond the grid.

The situated narratives that provide accounts from different seasons demonstrate how spatial inequalities and changes in energy practices play out over time. Seasonal dimensions and religious periods continue to shape not just food growing and consumption practices but also how modern energy is used for heating and cooling over the course of the year.

As such the chapter further highlights intersecting dynamics of people's lived experience with energy. It therefore demonstrates the need for a more integrated and situated approach to understanding metabolic process related to energy access.

Notes

1 In 2015 the use of plastic bags was officially banned in The Gambia (Singhateh, 2017). In Kartong there has consequently been a visible reduction in plastic litter strewn across the settlement but it has not stopped the use of disposable packaging and other short-lived goods. The resulting waste is disposed of on several landfills in the village.
2 There is no deposit on the bottles. She simply has loyal customers who return the empty bottles for her to re-use or she buys new bottles from Brikama when she runs out. Bottles are also increasingly sought after by other women in Kartong who engage in the juice-making business.
3 A few years ago, there was a trial to use cardboard in one of the smokehouses but the initiative was short lived.
4 The term ablution describes the washing of body parts including mouth, hands and feet before prayer.
5 Traditionally, it is not permitted to wash clothes in the centre of a courtyard which is, however, where the washing line and communal water tap are located.
6 Comment on 'Kartong weeklynews' Facebook post, 10 June 2018.
7 The last period of sand mining in Kartong which took place in 2015 ended with thirty-three youth including one woman being arrested, following protests against the mining activity. The conflict drew huge media attention across The Gambia and the Gambian diaspora living overseas. The 'Kartong 33' were eventually released and charges dropped (Jeffang, 2015).
8 The 'back way' is a common turn of phrase to describe the refugee route Gambians take to look for brighter futures in Europe.

References

Adair-Rohani, H., Zukor, K., Bonjour, S., Wilburn, S., Kuesel, A.C., Hebert, R. and Fletcher, E.R. (2013) Limited electricity access in health facilities of sub-Saharan Africa: A systematic review of data on electricity access, sources, and reliability. *Global Health: Science and Practice*, 1 (2), pp. 249–261. https://doi.org/10.9745/GHSP-D-13-00037

Conrad Suso, C.T. (2019) Backway or bust: Causes and consequences of Gambian irregular migration. *The Journal of Modern African Studies*, 57, pp. 111–135. https://doi.org/10.1017/S0022278X18000666

Jeffang, K. (2015) State withdraws all 5 charges against the Kartong 33. *Foroyaa* [Online], 2 December. Available from: <http://foroyaa.gm/state-withdraws-all-5-charges-against-the-kartong-33/> [Accessed 9 October 2019].

Munro, P.G. and Schiffer, A. (2019) Ethnographies of electricity scarcity: Mobile phone charging spaces and the recrafting of energy poverty in Africa. In: *Energy and buildings*, in press. https://doi.org/10.1016/j.enbuild.2019.01.038

Owili, P.O., Muga, M.A., Pan, W.-C. and Kuo, H.-W. (2017) Cooking fuel and risk of under-five mortality in 23 Sub-Saharan African countries: A population-based study. *International Journal of Environmental Health Research*, 27 (3), pp. 191–204. https://doi.org/10.1080/09603123.2017.1332347

Pfeiffer, B. and Mulder, P. (2013) Explaining the diffusion of renewable energy technology in developing countries. *Energy Economics*, 40, pp. 285–296. https://doi.org/10.1016/j.eneco.2013.07.005

Schiffer, A. (2016) Empowered, excited, or disenfranchised? Unveiling issues of energy access inequality and resource dependency in the Gambia. *Energy Research & Social Science*, 18 August, pp. 50–61. https://doi.org/10.1016/j.erss.2016.04.011

Schwerhoff, G. and Sy, M. (2017) Financing renewable energy in Africa: Key challenge of the sustainable development goals. *Renewable and Sustainable Energy Reviews*, 75, pp. 393–401.

Singhateh, M. (2017) Gambia: NEA issues warning on the sale of plastic bags. *Foroyaa* [Online], 16 November. Available from: <https://allafrica.com/stories/201711170400.html> [Accessed 9 October 2019].

Wu, B., Schiffer, A. and Burns, B. (2016) *Power for the people: Delivering decentralized, community-controlled renewable energy access*. Washington, Edinburgh, New York: ActionAid USA, Friends of the Earth Scotland, Women's Environment & Development Organization.

5 Enough is enough
Considering energy sufficiency

The previous chapters highlighted the fact that in Kartong technology leap-frogging has not occurred to meet increasing demands for electricity and that access and associated benefits are distributed unequally across society. Some households currently struggle to meet these demands whereas others are likely already over-consuming due to the use of energy-hungry appliances or wasteful practices. In response, this chapter explores how social practices are, or could be used to negotiate access to sufficient energy. I presented earlier thinking on energy sufficiency at the 2nd International Conference on Energy, Environment and Climate Change in Mauritius in 2017. It also fed into a position paper for Friends of the Earth International (FoEI), (Cadena et al., 2016), FoEI webinars in February and March 2017 and the FoEI People Power Now manifesto which was launched during the 24th Conference of the Parties to the UNFCCC in December 2018. The latter included a specific ask calling for 'energy sufficiency for all.'[1]

Basic energy is not sufficient

According to the IEA (2019) 860 million people in the world currently remain without access to electricity. Estimates suggest that by 2030, 650 million people will still be without access, most of whom (9 out of 10) will be in sub-Saharan Africa (IEA et al., 2019). In contrast, industrialised countries need to reduce overall energy consumption to drastically curb climate change emissions. Somewhere between these extremes of global under- and overconsumption lies what can be described as energy sufficiency.

The Gambia's Electricity Act 2005 (p. 5) aims to "ensure sufficient and reliable electricity" supply which is arguably a human right (Tully, 2006; What Next Forum et al., 2015, p. 2). In turn, this requires us to move beyond a mere moral stance and consider what sufficient energy means in practice (Darby, 2007). One of the issues is that energy access is often referred to in absolutes as suggested by the aforementioned IEA statistic. Either people have it or they do not. Yet, as earlier chapters have highlighted, people in Kartong had access to electricity in the form of batteries to power radios or electric lights and electricity to charge phones long before grid infrastructure reached Kartong. Instead of energy absolutes, a more nuanced understanding of energy scarcity is needed where it is possible to have *some* access to electricity (Munro and Schiffer, 2019).

Having access to some energy is however not necessarily the same as having sufficient access. Overcoming energy scarcity often emphasises access to lighting as being of particular importance for development because it enables people to study at night. However, previous chapters illustrate that Kartong also has a long history of non-electrical alternatives to lighting including firewood, kerosene lamps, candles and moonlight which were later replaced or used in parallel to various forms of battery powered lamps. During frequent periods of load shedding and in underserved parts of the settlement area, people continue to rely on some of these alternatives. This is not to suggest that a room poorly lit by a candle provides good conditions for studying, it merely serves to point out that different forms of lighting have been available for a long time and are therefore not necessarily a key priority for every household. Furthermore, a far greater barrier to education is posed by the fact that male school attendance was (and in some cases still is) prioritised over that of females, coupled with the burden of household chores that would have prevented girls from studying with or without access to light. Here, access to better lighting would have made little difference for women and girls. It would not have helped farming families overcome economic challenges to pay for education or changed the fact that most sons had more free time during daylight hours to study. Also, singular naked electric bulbs which are suspended from ceilings today in otherwise dark rooms do not necessarily provide good lighting for reading and writing either.

Nonetheless, according to the IEA (2017) "initial access to sufficient electricity to power a basic bundle of energy services" includes "at a minimum, several lightbulbs, task lighting (such as a flashlight), phone charging and a radio." A household solar installation could make that happen and for very limited gadgets miniature solar panels can provide small amounts of electricity (Figure 5.1). However, I strongly argue that sufficient energy goes beyond providing basic energy needs. Observations from the Indian context suggest that "even the most successful experiments are built on limited opportunity models – such as the lantern or the solar panel with a few lightbulbs, which works when people are poor. It does not meet needs or aspirations as people become richer or have more energy needs. In this way, existing solar energy systems have been designed only for the poor and only when they are poor (Bhushan and Kumar, 2012, p. iv)." Changes to energy

Figure 5.1 Miniature solar panel charging a mobile phone and rechargeable light

practices associated with the arrival of grid electricity in Kartong clearly demonstrate that energy provision needs to go beyond such limited opportunity models. Here, electricity is not merely used to generate income or study at night. People also want to watch television, use fans to keep cool during the rainy season, upgrade to household gadgets such as electric irons and kettles or run fridges for the purpose of small entrepreneurial enterprises.

If people's aspirations and future needs are not considered as part of designing energy access, infrastructure is likely to become redundant when it fails to provide access to sufficient energy and households revert to traditional energy practices such as the burning of wood fuels (Dlamini et al. 2016). In Kartong, the solar panels that served the central borehole became obsolete when a new pump was installed, despite the fact that the panels were only a few years old. The same is likely to happen at household level infrastructure. For example, when electricity fails or is unavailable for lighting, batteries, candles or firewood is used instead. Therefore, basic energy as set out by the IEA is not likely to provide sufficient energy, nor does it necessarily offer what is perceived to be important by local people. Greater and context-specific insight into everyday practices, including people's needs and preferences, is therefore essential.

While the IEA (2017) defines energy sufficiency in basic energy terms, it does also recognise that there needs to be capability to grow consumption over time. It projects that:

> the average household who has gained access has enough electricity to power four lightbulbs operating at five hours per day, one refrigerator, a fan operating 6 hours per day, a mobile phone charger and a television operating 4 hours per day, which equates to an annual electricity consumption of 1 250 kWh per household with standard appliances, and 420 kWh with efficient appliances.

Not long ago, this would have broadly chimed with appliances that could be found in newly grid-connected households in Kartong. However, the rapid uptake of electric gadgets means consumption is quickly exceeding this. A family that a few years ago only had one phone to charge and used candles or battery powered lamps now has a ceiling fan, three standing fans, a television set, five interior and four exterior lightbulbs, a washing machine, an electric iron, a small fridge and two mobile phones.[2] In addition the wife operates two large fridges for her juice business while the length of time some of these appliances are operated varies greatly and may far exceed the IEA's definition.

Limiting overconsumption

As previously mentioned, in industrialised parts of the world, the challenge of becoming energy sufficient is generally about reducing overall consumption with fuel-poor households as a notable exception (Thomas et al.,

2015). The opposite is true in contexts that are developing first-time access to modern energy services to reduce energy scarcity. Here, overall energy consumption needs to increase to enable "dignified" living conditions (Wu et al., 2016, p. 15; Tully, 2006). In Kartong and between neighbouring communities, widespread electricity scarcity prevails, largely due to the unequal distribution of grid infrastructure. As one Kartonka put it, when you hear that Kartong, the last village in The Gambia before the Senegalese border has electricity access, you do not imagine that the village before has been skipped. Yet, the village of Madina Salam has electricity infrastructure running through it but was itself never connected while its three neighbours of Kartong, Gunjur and Berending all received a number of household connections.

Musango et al. (2017, p. 6) point out: "It is important to be aware of the misconception that many cities of the global South appear to be resource efficient already, as this is largely due to unmet demands that have serious negative consequences for the poor." Arguably, the same applies to more rural areas in the hinterland of larger urban centres. While there are societies across the world that live contentedly off the land, energy sufficiency needs to challenge notions that people in developing countries generally have no desire to consume more or that they are satisfied when their basic energy needs are met. At some point in the future, Madina Salam, the remainder of Kartong and other villages in the region will likely gain full access to grid electricity to meet demand.

The IEA (2017) also estimates a large difference between households that use standard appliances and those that use more efficient ones. The latter consume almost two thirds less energy.[3] In The Gambia, this could therefore impact on greenhouse gas emissions associated with fossil-fuel–based electricity generation. It could also lead to a reduction in the running cost of appliances in a context where the unit cost of electricity is comparable with that of the UK but household incomes are substantially lower. Domestic energy reduction through efficiency measures that enable doing more with less would potentially increase chances for remaining households in Kartong or Madina Salam to be connected, relieving some of the pressure to meet demand. For example, what if households in the densely populated parts of Kartong were constructed in a way that they were less likely to overheat during the hot and humid rainy season, thereby reducing the need to run electric fans (Sonko and Wang, 2017)? More efficient practices would enable distribution to more households within the limits of available generating capacity at national level.

However, running more efficient gadgets means it may also increase the number of appliances a household is able to use. This phenomenon of increasing consumption when equipment or processes become more affordable with growing efficiency is known as 'Jevons paradox' or 'rebound effect' (Polimeni et al., 2008). A "positive "rebound effect"" may occur where energy efficiency measures, such as widespread adaptation of efficient appliances, lead to an increase and therefore sufficient level of energy consumed in households which were previously energy scarce (Jenkins et al., 2011).

Yet, when developing energy access, energy efficiency (let alone sufficiency) as a strategy to avoid future overconsumption is rarely talked about beyond the installation of energy saving lightbulbs. In fact, The Gambia's National Energy Efficiency Action Plan foresees "100% penetration of energy efficient lighting in on and off-grid systems" by 2020 and energy efficient lightbulbs are generally the norm in Kartong (Ceesay, 2015). However, beyond that, thinking about how to deliver energy access that considers how to avoid future overconsumption is not normally a priority when there is urgent demand to ensure people gain access to modern energy services in the first place.

Furthermore, instead of emphasising 'enoughness,' sufficiency can evoke connotations of 'backwardness' and solutions which are 'second best' (Princen, 2005). Here, for people like myself whose positionality classifies them as white Westerners, from countries that have historically and are still contributing significantly more to climate change, it is uncomfortable to suggest developing countries should limit their future consumption. What if someone thinks of us as imperialists?

Finally, sufficiency policies may be unpopular with the electorate and incompatible with the 'orthodox economic growth' paradigm in which policies focus on ever-growing economies through perpetually increasing consumption (Hennicke et al., 2014; Barry, 2012, 2015). The dominant economic system is in conflict with our 'ecologically constrained word' (Princen, 2005).

Nonetheless, "an increase in resource efficiency alone leads to nothing, unless it goes hand in hand with an intelligent restraint of growth" and "the opposite of poverty is not wealth, but sufficiency" (Sachs, 1999, p. 41; Seabrook, 2007, p. 46). By the same token, the opposite of energy scarcity is not unlimited access to modern energy services but access to sufficient energy. As such the concept of energy sufficiency challenges both the idea of basic energy as being enough for people in poverty as well as access to unrestricted levels of consumption. In The Gambia, a combination of restricting energy beyond the point of sufficient consumption and increasing especially local renewable energy generation to meet demand is likely needed.[4] Yet, what does energy sufficiency look like in practice?

The Isle of Eigg, which is located off the west coast of Scotland, is well known for its stand-alone mini-grid which is powered by a combination of small hydro, small wind and solar electricity with a diesel generator back-up. Approximately 95% of electricity needed by the 100 or so people who live on the island is derived from the combination of renewables (Eigg Electric, n.d).

However, before Eigg Electric became operational in 2008, the islanders largely relied on diesel generators that would produce electricity for a limited amount of hours a day, a scenario that is all too familiar to many West Africans. Shipping fossil fuels to the island's small ferry terminal and transporting it from there to individual households was expensive, time consuming and cumbersome. A connection to the mainland grid was not feasible. Eventually, the community managed to secure funding in the region of £1.6 million (US$2 million; €1.9 million) to install the mini-grid and local generating capacity to provide round-the-clock affordable electricity. Finance came largely from European Union funding while residents contributed £500 (US$620; €580) per household and £1,000 (US$1,250; €1,160) per business connection.

Usually more generating capacity is needed to compensate for peak consumption times though infrastructure may not be needed for the remainder of the day. In order to keep overall capital cost down, islanders had to find a way to avoid these consumption spikes in their system. They therefore decided to implement a consumption cap of 5kW for households and 10kW for businesses. If a household (or business) turns on too many electrical appliances at the same time and goes over this threshold, it is automatically disconnected from the island grid (Eigg Electric, 2009). A local engineer then has to physically come out and reconnect said household. This inconvenience acts as a great deterrent.

To manage their consumption, households and businesses were initially provided with a small portable display unit that indicates near–real-time power consumption intended to help islanders stay under the 5kW/10kW cap. However, conversations with local people and observations suggest that many have become so used to the set-up that they no longer require the aid of the monitors and intuitively know when they are close to the consumption limit.[5] Some have developed unique behaviour patterns to manage the constraints of the system. For example, one resident leaves a small object on the base of an electric kettle to warn that turning the kettle on would lead the household to breach the threshold when a series of other appliances are in use.

The consumption cap has forced islanders to adapt their behaviours in the process of moving from underconsumption of energy to live with a sufficient amount of power, providing an example of a community that is practising energy sufficiency. Importantly sufficiency behaviour was integrated from the onset, not as an afterthought.

The set-up is of course not directly transferable to The Gambia, where climate, practices and geography are very different. Nonetheless, a similar regional approach that limits consumption in principle could help to manage finite supply more equitably.

Sufficiency as a behavioural approach

One of the differences between efficiency and sufficiency approaches is that the former is focused on technological optimisation whereas the latter is more concerned with behaviour (Toulouse et al., 2017). However, the two are closely linked. In Kartong ongoing water supply issues demonstrate what happens when sufficiency behaviour is not considered.

For about two decades Kartong has had access to water from a central borehole. Initially European funding paid for the system including solar photovoltaics that generated electricity to pump water from the borehole into a tank raised several meters above ground. From there, water was distributed using gravitational force through a network of pipes and public taps. With a growing population, plus the need for repair and limited generating capacity, the system was unable to meet increasing demand. During the 2013 rainy season, valves that release the water from the tank were only opened once every two weeks, leaving people to rely mainly on household wells instead (Schiffer, 2016).

Shortly after, a donation by Dutch sponsors enabled an upgrade of the system which included a new lining for the storage tank and solar panels. With an extension of pipes to more recent parts of the settlement area, people in Kartong had for the first time access to piped, clean drinking water 24 hours a day. Water supply had been completely transformed and Kartong had a stand-alone 100% renewable electricity powered system which provided water sovereignty. The VDC set up a water committee which experimented with strategies to raise finance and ensure the community would be able to maintain the system.

However, more and more compounds paid to have private taps connected to the network. Taps are either located in a central part of extended family compounds or occasionally in individual households (or back gardens) hidden from public view. It did not take long before the water supply system reached its limits as consumption soared. Once again, the flow of water from the tank was rationed to several hours a day. Improved access to solar energy quickly contributed to increased consumption of local water, limited by the size of the storage tank and the availability of electricity to power the pump. There was no incentive to consume water within the means available because increased consumption did not relate to an increased amount of monthly fees that were initially required but became more and more difficult to enforce. Instead, people, including those that would leave their own taps running with buckets overflowing, started to complain about neighbours who used their taps to water vegetable gardens or banana plants.

As a result, the water committee considered connecting the system to the NAWEC grid to buy in additional power which eventually took place in early 2019. However, in the process a more powerful pump was installed which is not compatible with the solar panels which were consequently disconnected. Since then, installation fees for new private taps and donations from Gambians including those living abroad are paying for grid electricity to keep the system going. It should be noted that remittance payments are a common form of financial support in The Gambia, accounting for an estimated 20% of Gross Domestic Product (World Bank Group, 2018). Nonetheless, it is unlikely to provide a viable long-term solution. At the time of writing, the water committee is working towards the installation of household meters to ensure that people pay for what they consume in the hope that this will reduce the overall demand for water. The installation cost will have to be covered by individual households.

The preceding example demonstrates that in Kartong the lack of a particular piece of technological equipment – a water meter – enabled behaviour that was not in line with sufficiency. This quickly led to overconsumption and wastage. Not having considered sufficient behaviour and equitable distribution when the system was initially upgraded led to the move away from renewable energy to the adaptation of fossil-fuel–based power to supply water. It is essentially the opposite of leapfrogging, further cementing Kartong's growing dependence on fossil fuels to provide local services.

Insufficient energy supply and infrastructure

Availability of grid electricity in Kartong depends on limited national generating capacity which is currently unable to meet demand. In March 2018 the country commissioned a floating fossil-fuelled generator or 'energy ship' to add additional generating capacity (Jeffang, 2018). This further emphasises how at a national level The Gambia is not leapfrogging to renewables to meet increasing demand. Saying that, temporary infrastructure can be more easily replaced with renewables in the future than static power stations which comprise the majority of the generating capacity in the country.

Due to the lack of capacity, end users continue to experience load shedding. Subsequently, even the parts of Kartong which are electrified currently do not have access to constant electricity. The length of time per day electricity is available is a factor that should therefore be included in defining energy sufficiency for The Gambia. However, '24/7 access' and 'reliable access' to sufficient energy might not be the same thing (De Decker, 2018).

During my last visit to Kartong in July 2019, it seemed electricity could go off at any time making it more difficult for households to manage their consumption, impacting on the central water supply and causing a general sense of frustration, exacerbated by the fact that it is experienced as unpredictable. Here, load shedding becomes especially noticeable as electric lights, sewing machines and televisions suddenly switch off. Load shedding is not just a concern in The Gambia but affects the wider region including countries such as Ghana, Zambia and South Africa (Gyamfi et al., 2018; Dlamini et al., 2016). Caps that flatten consumption peaks could potentially make it easier to provide load shedding timetables that are acceptable to the general public and therefore part of providing sufficient energy.

Regardless of load shedding, Kartong is officially electrified. However, years after electrification, there are clearly visible access inequalities across the community which shape energy practices differently between households that are grid connected and those that are not. Even a recent influx of off-grid solar photovoltaic installations does not provide an adequate alternative as they fail to be maintained and/or meet demand.

When grid electricity first arrived in Kartong during the 2013 rainy season this coincided with the end of Ramadan. Muslims in Kartong were preparing for *Koriteh*, the celebration that marks the end of the fasting period which is associated with increased expenses as people pay for new clothing or animals to be slaughtered as part of religious festivities. Simultaneously, the rainy season is characterised by reduced income as families lose seasonal employment in the tourist industry and focus on growing rice. In Kartong, this contributed to only a relatively small number of nineteen households being able to afford to pay the grid connection fee and cover necessary additional costs for smaller poles or brackets required, depending on the proximity to the nearest NAWEC pole (Schiffer, 2016). In other words, access to electricity infrastructure was limited by economic capabilities to raise necessary funds which in turn was strongly influenced by seasonal dimensions. In Sambou Kunda, one part of the compound could afford the initial connection fee and immediately installed electric lighting and a television satellite dish. The remainder continued to rely on candles and battery powered torches as did the majority of Kartong's population at the time.

Over the following year more and more households across the community, including the remaining households in Sambou Kunda, managed to save up money to pay the connection fee and become 'electrified.' Today the vast majority of compounds along the grid in Kartong have access to electricity. Yet, what is known locally as 'phase one' of rural electrification that reached Kartong over half a decade ago has over time resulted in substantial differences in household energy practices across the settlement. Here, it should be noted that this spatial inequality also disadvantages the majority of the Balanta ethnic group that live in Balanta Kunda, a cluster of households located behind the football field just beyond the edge of the grid.

However, some suggest that back in 2013 NAWEC had limited capacity to make more connections despite there being more households who could have raised sufficient funds. Similarly, it would be erroneous to assume that many of the households that currently live beyond grid coverage would not be able to afford connection if the grid extended to their part of the settlement. For now, these have the option to privately pay for grid extension poles at an approximate cost of around D25,000–30,000 (€440–530; US$500–600) per unit in addition to several thousand dalasi required for brackets or smaller household poles as well as meters for which the price has gone up since the first installations in Kartong were made. The farther households are located from the grid, the more extension poles and the larger the sum that is required. This further exacerbates existing spatial inequalities. An exception are households of individuals who benefit due to their positions in government or NAWEC which automatically result in extensions being brought to their compounds. Apart from this, only a few wealthier households such as those owned by Westerners have the economic capability to pay the large sums required to get connected.

Considering gender in energy sufficiency

In Kartong energy practices remain highly gendered. As such, it is important to consider sufficient access not just at community or household level, but also from the perspective of individuals. Women are more likely to be excluded from some of the benefits associated with modern energy services. In Kartong, women are excluded, disadvantaged or adversely affected in several ways. Firstly, due to the fact that women's education has been given less priority, they experience higher levels of illiteracy. Women are therefore less able to independently use ICTs such as mobile phones to read and write messages, carry out searches using mobile internet or perform other tasks that require literacy skills. To a lesser extent, illiterate older men are excluded in a similar way (Schiffer, 2016). Recently, this has started to be mitigated somewhat with smart phone applications such as WhatsApp that enable voice recording.

Secondly, in relation to practices surrounding food some changes have occurred, namely the use of kettles and fridges that provide convenience or enable informal businesses such as the sale of juice. However, cooking facilities themselves, which traditionally remain the domain of women, have not been majorly replaced by electric or other alternatives that would improve women's health which continues to be impacted by indoor air pollution. The extent to which women in Kartong suffer adverse health impacts associated with cooking requires further investigation. Yet observations of women and their personal accounts suggest it is a common problem. One woman living on the edge of Kartong was told by her doctor to avoid cooking over charcoal and firewood because it was causing her significant breathing issues. Now her daughter is responsible for cooking chores instead.

Thirdly, a broader perspective on energy which links food production and transport highlights that women gardeners were affected by the loss of arable land close to the settlement area caused by repeated periods of sand mining which was itself enabled by improvements in road infrastructure. There is a great overlap between older women who are illiterate and excluded from the benefits of ICTs and those that grow vegetables and sell foods on informal roadside stalls to support their livelihoods.

However, it should be noted that in recent years more and more young girls can now be seen cycling along the road, either on their way to school, or just for fun, which is changing gendered transport practices. Similarly, more women are driving private cars in Kartong as they visit family from the urban centres or drive to the river to pick up fish for lunch. As an elder suggests, education and awareness have led to these changes (P11).

Gender-responsive policies and governance structures are increasingly recognised in wider debates as important in delivering sustainable energy access for all (Wu et al., 2016). Also, the impact that non-energy policies such as education have on everyday energy practices carries great importance (Butler et al., 2018; Royston et al., 2018; Greene, 2020). However, in practical terms women's voices in energy-related decision making are still lacking, especially in patriarchal societies where women's roles are focused on childcare and looking after the home (Cadena et al., 2018). For example, "grid extension programmes have often ignored gender inequalities seeing households as an ungendered unit" (Practical Action, 2018, p. 66).

Sharing as sufficiency strategy

While there are stark access inequalities in Kartong, for a long time, access to resources has also been negotiated through the socio-cultural practice of sharing. Older Kartonkas recall being self-sufficient in terms of food resources, but this was somewhat precarious due to seasonal fluctuations and insufficiency being stigmatised as what happens to those who are lazy. Nonetheless, when households experienced food shortages, this was mitigated by the wider community where extended family and friendship networks looked after one another. To this day, the sharing of food and food preparation is an important socio-cultural practice that can be observed across Kartong. Families and friends eat from the same large bowl during lunch, women share responsibilities to cook for extended family living together, or gather to prepare large quantities of food during celebrations such as naming ceremonies, weddings and religious festivities. During one of my visits, the former president had donated a truckload of groundnuts to the village to be sown which was deposited in the courtyard of the alkalo's compound. Before the groundnuts were taken to the fields, their shells had to be cracked by hitting them onto the ground. Every woman in Kartong had to crack at least one bowl full of nuts, sharing the workload.

In a sense, even children are being shared. As illustrated in Chapter 2, some elders remember growing up with childless relatives to provide additional labour. Today, it is still common for children to live for prolonged periods of time with relatives, sometimes for schooling, other times to strengthen family ties including relationships that span the Gambia Casamance border. Similarly, some of the co-wife relationships stem from the fact that brothers of deceased husbands offer to take responsibility for looking after their brother's widows and respective children. These and other examples, including the emphasis put on greeting rituals, are integral to values associated with communal life that underpin Kartong society to this day.

As such, it is unsurprising that sharing practices can also be observed in the ways in which access to modern energy services are negotiated. Previously, the mobile phone charging business disappeared almost overnight when grid electricity reached the community, despite only a small number of households being connected initially (Munro and Schiffer, 2019). The charging business has only reappeared recently to serve migrant workers who lack the social ties within the community.

Others are overcoming the spatial and economic divide between the settlement areas that live on and off the grid through temporary installations. On the occasion of a naming ceremony in Balanta Kunda, the closest house connected to the grid provided access via a series of extension leads lying in the grass along the edge of the football field. For the short period of time that electricity was especially needed, it was sufficiently met through this temporary connection. On a smaller scale, a kettle in Sambou Kunda was shared between several households and moved throughout the compound as and when needed, at least until it broke down. Similarly, a young tailor who is currently renting rooms in the compound for his business is invited to lunch. He can also choose between different Sambou Kunda households to watch television in the evenings, thereby accessing fixed appliances.

In a similar fashion, a man who technically resides in Kartong and whose employment guaranteed him electricity access through an extension to his compound, frequently travels and therefore rarely uses one of the three meters installed (the others are used by his extended family). He offered to put in an underground cable to connect the spare meter to a neighbour's compound who would otherwise not have benefitted from grid electricity.

This demonstrates that sufficient energy needs in Kartong can arguably be met as a condition of strong social relations in which energy resources and services are shared. Therefore, in the context of unequally distributed access, sufficient energy of one household has to take into account that it is compensating for the lack of access in others. The quantitative estimates of household needs by the IEA of "a mobile phone charger and a television set operating for 4 hours a day" becomes untenable where most households are also providing energy to friends, relatives and neighbours (IEA, 2017). In practice, the tailor who does not have his own television will come by late into the night to watch an action movie without disturbance when others have gone to bed. Similarly, phone charging is not limited to the people who live in a particular household and smaller appliances are shared across compounds.

However, while sharing practices are an integral part of the social fabric of Kartong and shape how energy access is negotiated locally, it is not a silver bullet. One barrier is a self-reported sense of jealousy over what others have. In extreme cases there are suspicions that some of the smaller bush fires which have destroyed people's orchards in recent times have been lit on purpose whilst individuals express joy over other's misfortune. Jealously is also said to have caused tensions over one of the recent electricity grid extensions: a Gambian living abroad made a donation to cover the cost of several extension poles, benefiting members of his family and nearby neighbours. However, two neighbouring compounds happened to apply for a meter through a different NAWEC branch to the donor's family and it just so happened that these arrived and were installed first. Feeling that this was unfair because it was their family's connection who paid for the poles, the donor's family complained to the point that the neighbours decided to have their meters taken down until the donor's family received their connection.

This could have been the end, however the situation further escalated involving different parties having to appear for police interviews over things that may or may not have been said, a pet dog being injured and ultimately the total breakdown in relationship between members of the donor's family and their neighbours. When a woman belonging to the donor's family decided to enter one of the neighbour's compounds and hang her washing as she had previously done, she was told to take it down and leave. The neighbours involved all decided to stop sharing their resources including access to a well and the fence where she had previously hung her washing.

Furthermore, socio-cultural expectations around sharing can also place a heavy burden on individuals. Elders recall the pressure on people who in the past owned one of few bicycles or cars in the community. In the same way, a Kartonka recalls that he briefly opened a shop selling food to improve his household income. However, when a local woman came to buy rice and did not have enough money to pay for it, he would not only feel compelled to give her rice on credit, he also provided her with cash so that she could buy vegetables or fish in the market. As a result, major shops in Kartong are largely owned by immigrants from other West and North African countries who do not experience this kind of social pressure that pose a burden on locals.

Finally, sharing what is mine with friends and relatives is not the same as taking collective responsibility for infrastructure and associated costs. As a Kartonka said to me while we were standing under the remains of a rattling windmill that once served as a water pump before the central borehole with its solar system was installed (Figure 5.2): "if everybody owns it, no one cares." The newer central borehole has a long history of the community collectively struggling to take responsibility for maintenance. Similarly, Kartong's first electricity grid, which provided streetlights powered by a large diesel generator, became obsolete when shared fuel and maintenance costs were not met by the community. It is not to say that Kartong as a community does not have the willingness or capabilities to collectively look after infrastructure but that complex socio-cultural and socio-economic dimensions need to be carefully considered, especially where costs are involved.

Figure 5.2 Remnants of a wind-powered water pump that once served Kartong

Having to ask a friend, neighbour or relative to pay for a service such as maintenance fees despite knowing that the person is financially struggling, is strongly felt by individuals. Here, neutral governance structures that build on the socio-cultural practice of sharing whilst enabling collective responsibility could transform the way communities like Kartong manage local infrastructure.

Beyond energy sufficiency as a moral stance

Focusing on electricity, I have argued that in practical terms, access to sufficient energy goes beyond basic needs (such as lighting) being met whilst simultaneously advocating for consumption limits. Cropper (2008, p. 2) suggests that: "It will only be by a combination of resource efficiency and resource sufficiency measures that the ultimate goal of sustainable consumption and production patterns can be achieved." As such, efficiency and sufficiency policies do not necessarily oppose each other but can and should be integrated (Thomas et al., 2015). Here, one-size-fits-all definitions for what constitutes sufficiency are inappropriate as they fail to consider specific contextual factors and situated practices. In Kartong, infrastructural inequalities, seasonal differences, gender and sharing practices all shape energy access on the ground.

Can a household be deemed as having access to sufficient electricity if sudden load shedding makes it difficult to manage consumption? What about illiterate women who theoretically have access to electricity and mobile phones but are unable to use information technologies the same way a literate person might? Can we really say that they have access to sufficient energy or is it like arguing that a person who owns the car parked outside has therefore access to sufficient transport when she has never learnt to drive?

While I purposefully refrain from offering a quantitative definition, I expect that in the context of Kartong and the wider Kombo South District of The Gambia, sufficient levels of electricity consumption should be more in line with the example of the household I provided towards the beginning of this chapter. For energy scarce households, access to sufficient energy still needs to be achieved to meet developmental objectives and a limit to consumption also needs to be explored if the aim is to live sustainably in the future. However, strong social ties need to be considered through which otherwise energy-scarce households negotiate access in a communal context of infrastructural inequalities. In turn, this requires "sufficiency oriented politics" and policies that put greater emphasis on the lived experience of energy access developments (Schneidewind and Zahrnt, 2014). Only then will sufficiency move from a moral stance towards a guiding 'principle' informing practice (Princen, 2005).

Notes

1 The FoEI People Power Now manifesto can be accessed at: www.foei.org/wp-content/uploads/2018/11/14-FoEI-PPN-manifesto-ENG-lr.pdf
2 It should also be noted that some people have two phones to compensate for the intermittent service of different network providers or to get the best deal. Some people use dual-sim phones, others frequently switch between sim cards.
3 Grid efficiencies and losses are not taken into account here.
4 There are plans to develop large-scale solar generation and storage capacity in The Gambia (Bellini, 2019).
5 I visited Eigg as part of my previous role as energy campaigner for Friends of the Earth Scotland (Schiffer, 2014).

References

Barry, J. (2015) Green political economy: Beyond orthodox undifferentiated economic growth as a permanent feature of the economy. In: Gabrielson, T., et al. eds. *Oxford handbook of environmental political theory*. Oxford: Oxford University Press, pp. 304–317.

Barry, J. (2012) *The politics of actually existing unsustainability: Human flourishing in a climate changed, carbon constrained world*. Oxford: Oxford University Press.

Bellini, E. (2019) Gambia plans 150 MW solar project with 20 MWh storage option. *PV Magazine* [Online], 1 October. Available from: <www.pv-magazine.com/2019/10/01/gambia-plans-150-mw-solar-project-with-20-mwh-storage-option/> [Accessed 10 October 2019].

Bhushan, C. and Kumar, J. (2012) *Going remote: Re-inventing the off-grid solar revolution for clean energy for all*. New Delhi: Centre for Science and Environment.

Butler, C., Parkhill, K.A. and Luzecka, P. (2018) Rethinking energy demand governance: Exploring impact beyond "energy" policy. *Energy Research and Social Science*, 36, pp. 70–78.

Cadena, L., Broom, F., Ali, A., Bhatnagar, D., Shaw, S. and Schiffer, A. (2018) *People, power, now: An energy manifesto*. Amsterdam: Friends of the Earth International.

Cadena, L., Schiffer, A. and Shaw, S. (2016) *Energy: Access and sufficiency: Enough is enough: Understanding "energy sufficiency" as an integral part of delivering energy access* [briefing]. Amsterdam: Friends of the Earth International.

Ceesay, K.K. (2015) Sustainable energy action plan for the Gambia [presentation]. *ECOWAS Sustainable Energy Policy and High Level Forum, September 15, 2015*. Abidjan.

Cropper, A. (2008) Decoupling economic growth from environmental degradation: The crucial role of resource efficiency. *Green Week Conference, June 3–6, 2008*. Brussels. Available from: <http://ec.europa.eu/environment/archives/green week2008/sources/pres/opening_angela_cropper.pdf> [Accessed 21 September 2019].

Darby, S. (2007) *Enough is as good as a feast: Sufficiency as policy*. Oxford: Oxford University Press.

De Decker, K. (2018) Keeping some of the lights on: Redefining energy security [Online article]. *Low-Tech Magazine*. Available from: <www.lowtechmagazine.

com/2018/12/keeping-some-of-the-lights-on-redefining-energy-security.html> [Accessed 23 September 2019].

Dlamini, C., Moombe, K.B., Syampungani, S. and Samboko, P.C. (2016) Load shedding and charcoal use in Zambia: What are the implications on forest resources? [Working paper]. Lusaka, Indaba Agricultural Policy Research Institute.

Eigg Electric (n.d.) *Eigg electric* [Online]. Isle of Eigg: Eigg Electric. Available from: <http://isleofeigg.org/eigg-electric/> [Accessed 21 November 2019].

Eigg electric: Renewable energy for the Isle of Eigg (2009) [Online video]. Available from: <www.youtube.com/watch?v=l3n-6YHquno> [Accessed 21 September 2019].

Electricity Act 2005 (c. 3) Banjul: State House.

Greene, M. and Fahy, F. (2020) Steering demand? Exploring the intersection of policy, practice and lives in energy systems change in Ireland. *Energy Research and Social Science*, 61. https://doi.org/10.1016/j.erss.2019.101331

Gyamfi, S., Diawuo, F.A., Kumi, E.N., Sika, F. and Modjinou, M. (2018) The energy efficiency situation in Ghana. *Renewable and Sustainable Energy Reviews*, 82 (1), pp. 1415–1423. https://doi.org/10.1016/j.rser.2017.05.007

Hennicke, P., Khosla, A., Dewan, C., Nagrath, K., Niazi, Z., O'Brien, M., Thakur, M.S. and Wilts, H. (2014) *Decoupling economic growth from resource consumption: A transformation strategy with manifold socio economic benefits for India and Germany*. Berlin: Deutsche Gesellschaft für Internationale Zusammenarbeit (GIZ) GmbH.

IEA (2019) *Energy access* [Online]. Paris: International Energy Agency. Available from: <www.iea.org/energyaccess/> [Accessed 21 November 2019].

IEA (2017) *Energy access Outlook 2017: Defining and modelling energy access*. Paris: International Energy Agency. Available from: <www.iea.org/media/pub lications/weo/EnergyAccessOutlook2017Definingandmodellingenergyaccess. pdf> [Accessed 21 September 2019].

IEA, IRENA, UNSD, WB and WHO (2019) *Tracking SDG 7: The energy progress report 2019*. Washington, DC: World Bank Publications.

Jeffang, K. (2018) Energy ship docks at Banjul Port. *Foroyaa* [Online], 14 March. Available from: <http://foroyaa.gm/energy-ship-docks-at-banjul-port/> [Accessed 21 September 2019].

Jenkins, D., Middlemiss, L. and Pharoah, R. (2011) *A study of fuel poverty and low-carbon synergies in social housing*. London: UKERC.

Munro, P.G. and Schiffer, A. (2019) Ethnographies of electricity scarcity: Mobile phone charging spaces and the recrafting of energy poverty in Africa. *Energy and Buildings*, 188–189, pp. 175–183. https://doi.org/10.1016/j.enbuild.2019.01.038

Musango, J.K., Currie, P. and Robinson, B. (2017) *Urban metabolism for resource efficient cities: From theory to implementation*. Paris: UN Environment.

Polimeni, J.M., Mayumi, K., Giampietro, M. and Alcott, B. (2008) *The Jevons paradox and the myth of resource efficiency improvements*. London, UK: Earthscan.

Practical Action (2018) *Poor people's energy outlook 2018: Achieving inclusive energy access at scale*. Rugby: Practical Action Publishing. https://doi. org/10.3362/9781780447544

Princen, T. (2005) *The logic of sufficiency*. Cambridge: MIT Press.

Royston, S., Selby, J. and Shove, E. (2018) Invisible energy policies: A new agenda for energy demand reduction. *Energy Policy*, 123, pp. 127–135. https://doi.org/10.1016/j.enpol.2018.08.052

Sachs, W. (1999) *Planet dialectics*. London: Zed Books.

Schiffer, A. (2016) Empowered, excited, or disenfranchised? Unveiling issues of energy access inequality and resource dependency in the Gambia. *Energy Resaarch & Social Science*, 18 August, pp. 50–61.

Schiffer, A. (2014) *From remote island grids to urban solar co-operatives*. Edinburgh: Friends of the Earth Scotland.

Schneidewind, U. and Zahrnt, A., (2014) The institutional framework for a sufficiency driven economy. *Ökologisches Wirtschaften*, 29, pp. 30–33. DOI: 10.14512/OEW290330

Seabrook, J. (2007) *The no-nonesense guide to world poverty*. 2nd ed. Oxford: New Internationalist Publications.

Sonko, S. and Wang, T.J. (2017) Mitigating high energy consumption for residential buildings in the Gambia. *34th International Symposium on Automation and Robotics in Construction (ISARC), June 28–July 1, 2017*. Bratislava: International Association for Automation and Robotics in Construction.

Thomas, S., Brischke, L.A., Thema, J. and Kopatz, M. (2015) Energy sufficiency policy: An evolution of energy efficiency policy or radical new approaches? In: *eceee Summer Study Proceedings: First Fuel Now, 1–6 June 2015, 2015*, Toulon/Hyères. Stockholm: European Council for Energy Efficiency, pp. 59–70.

Toulouse, E., Le Dû, M., Gorge, H. and Semal, L. (2017) Stimulating energy sufficiency: Barriers and opportunities. In: *eceee Summer Study Proceedings: Consumption, Efficiency and Limits, May 29–June 3, 2017*, Toulon/Hyères. Stockholm: European Council for Energy Efficiency, pp.59–68.

Tully, S. (2006) Access to electricity as human right. *Netherlands Quarterly of Human Rights*, 24 (4), pp. 557–588.

What Next Forum, Centre for Science and Environment and Friends of the Earth International (2015) *Programme for Global Renewable Energy and Energy Access Transformation (GREEAT)*. Uppsala: What Next Forum.

World Bank Group (2018) *Migration and remittance: Recent developments and Outlook*. Migration and Development Brief 29. Washington: World Bank Group.

Wu, B., Schiffer, A. and Burns, B. (2016) *Power for the people: Delivering decentralized, community-controlled renewable energy access*. Washington, DC: ActionAid USA, Friends of the Earth Scotland, Women's Environment & Development Organization.

6 Kartong energy futures
Chance for positive change

Previous chapters have explored the past and present of energy in Kartong, thereby drawing out a number of themes that have shaped its changing energy metabolism including gender dimensions, infrastructural development and socio-cultural practices such as sharing. In terms of energy sources, the transition towards modern energy services has been met through an increasingly linear energy metabolism highly dependent on fossil fuels to provide motorised transport, grid electricity and even water. Moving forward this suggests that to overcome energy scarcity and meet sufficient demands, Kartong and The Gambia at large will follow conventional development paths based on fossil fuel dependence, centralised power generation and the economic, social and environmental costs associated with this.

Chapter 6 explores current development trajectories in relation to people's aspirations for the future and sustainable development. Insight into people's aspirations has been developed as part of several co-design workshops with different stakeholder groups in Kartong which focused on moving from current practices to positive energy futures. These co-design workshops first took place in August 2013 with initial follow-up in January 2015. A local steering group provided guidance in shaping workshop content and recruiting participants. The group was largely comprised of Kartonkas involved in decision making at local level or had experience of public and third sector organisations. Additional workshops in July 2019 funded through the British Academy/Leverhulme Small Grant Scheme, contributed to a more recent perspective. These specifically focused on drawing out perceptions and aspirations of women and young adult men (male youth) whose voices are traditionally less present in decision making at community and other levels. Specifically, the chapter shares insights gathered through visioning exercises that were a shared component of all workshops since 2013. Appendix 1 includes a handout prepared for 2019 participants providing a more detailed outline of workshop activities and the underlying methodological framework.

Imagining complex energy futures can be daunting and feel removed from one's everyday life. To make things more tangible during the visioning exercises, participants in all workshops were instead asked to reflect on their personal experience and list complaints, something which tends to be easier for many people.[1] This took place in smaller groups in which each chose areas such as electricity, transport or cooking to create lists of negatives such as 'we don't want to be without street lights all over Kartong' or 'have bad cars that pollute the environment.' Only when groups had exhausted these negative lists were they asked to turn them into positive alternatives, thereby creating a vision for the future.

For the 2013 and 2015 workshop the steering group set a date of 2030 to work towards, in line with national and international policy targets and programmes. In contrast, participants in 2019 set their own timeline for when they wished their vision to be achieved by.

Envisioning food related practices

In 2013, participants had a broad discussion under the heading of 'heating,' which largely focused on cooking-related practices. They did not want these to be "difficult" referring to the labour intensity associated, for example, with collecting firewood or producing charcoal. However, it should also not be "expensive" and fuel sources "should not come from outside" Kartong land. Furthermore, practices should not pose a "health hazard" or be "environmentally unfriendly." Related to this, participants also said "fire should not be used for clearing agri[cultural] land." By 2030 participants envisioned "health hazard free and environmentally friendly" alternatives but offered little detail other than "it should [be achieved] by renewable energy."

In 2015 the group envisioned "food security" and for food to be "sufficient in the community" by 2030. Discussing health impacts and land use, the group wanted to "minimise using firewood" for cooking and instead "promote biogas cooking system[s]." To this day biogas has not become available in the community. Instead, some households rely on conventional gas for cooking meals as an alternative to firewood, despite the additional cost. However, analysis shows that "biogas has significant potential in the Gambia and can be made from animal waste as well as agricultural waste and sewage sludge" (SEforALL, 2012, p. 23). If it is not possible to produce biogas locally, supply could potentially build on existing trade networks of agri- and aquacultural produce to and from Brikama.

Participants also discussed land use more generally because of the clear links to food production, extraction of local biomass such as firewood as well as ongoing tensions over sand mining imposed on the community at that time. The group suggested "not to sell lands," but that local land should be for "lease or rent." There should also be "no mining" and "no deforestation." Instead, the group wanted to see "restoration" through "tree planting." Some of the discussion was about recent success in restoring of local mangrove forests along the Allahein river.

Furthermore, the group raised concerns over "external food dependency" and the use of chemicals in food production. Participants envisioned that emphasis should be put on "farming system[s]" which includes the need for a "storage facility." Finally, participants promoted "animal husbandry," addressing both destruction of vegetable gardens by roaming livestock and providing a sense of financial security as animals can be sold for profit in times of need. In relation to food production, the future was modelled on historic practices in Kartong, when the community was largely able to feed itself and livestock provided security as well as meat produce and other protein.

Fast forward to the rainy season in 2019 and it becomes evident that climate change is already leading to shorter growing cycles for staple crops such as rice. The changing climate also puts pressure on water resources available whilst increasing the risk of bushfires that affects fruit orchards and the wider local environment. As permanent secretary for agriculture and Kartonka Momodou Mbye Jabang says, reflecting on the increasing absence of rain, "we need to think outside the box."[2] While there are undoubtedly valuable lessons from the past, reverting to historic practices is unlikely to ensure resilient food production in the context of climate change.

During the 2019 workshops, women looked specifically at household energy. Discussions were largely focused on the use of electricity including gadgets such as kettles. However, in relation to major cooking practices, women complained about "stoves that consume[] lots of fuel." By 2021, they want to "use rocket stoves" and saw this as a priority. Similarly, male youth raised concerns over "[air] pollution from firewood" and wanted equipment to be "free from pollution" by 2021–25.

Male youth also expressed concerns over potential fires from candles being used "carelessly" to provide lighting as well as "unsafe . . . gas usage." Two participants recalled that one of them nearly burned his face when he went to light a gas burner not realising that the valve was left partially open and gas had escaped. They suspected that a child who had access tampered with the bottle.[3]

The future of transport

In 2013, workshop participants said they did not want to "have expensive means of transport." Instead, participants wanted "free transport" by 2030, though there was discussion that 'affordable' alternatives to cover travel to and from Kartong would be more realistic.

Regarding the quality of transport services provided, participants complained about "poor road networks" and "dirty road[s] for transport" which at the time was exacerbated by sand dropping off the back of trucks carrying locally extracted sand. They also objected to "large cars . . . to transport passengers," referring to commonly used bush taxis. By 2030 participants wanted "good and clean roads" and "small sizeable cars that are efficient."

Participants did not want to have "second hand cars," "bad cars that pollute the environment" or "vehicles that use [a] large quantity of fuel." Instead they envisioned that by 2030, motorised transport would be "free from pollution" and rely on "fuel efficient" or what participants described as "non-fuel cars," a term used here to refer to vehicles powered by solar energy.

Furthermore, there should be "no transportation by head," following a discussion about women in particular carrying heavy loads which should instead rely on adequate "equipment to transport materials" at local level. Finally, commonly used "timber canoes" should be replaced with "fibre glass canoes using [physical] work or solar power."

In 2015, workshop participants said they did not want "expensive cost of fuel" or "any pollution from car fumes." Instead, by 2030 "fuel cost should be affordable" and "there should be 0% pollution" emitted, for example by relying on renewable sources to power motorised vehicles. However, local land was recognised as the most valuable asset of the village and its people, especially in the context of Kartong promoting responsible tourism (KART, 2005). As such, "other renewable fuels should be preferable over biofuels." At that point, mobility for local journeys in and around Kartong was predominately based on walking and cycling, something that the group wanted to preserve, stating that "this group does not want motorised transport to overshadow local means of transportation."

Though not an issue in Kartong at the time, there was a concern over the potential adaptation of motorcycle taxis known as 'jakarta'[4] common in neighbouring Senegal. The group saw the value of motorcycle systems but wanted a "regulated replication of "motorbike taxis"" to ensure their safety.

Finally, "this group does not want unregulated motorised transport for fishing supply, tourism and river transport" which should also "be regulated." There was a particular concern over the impact of motorised river transport on local oyster fishing and specifically on the water quality in which oysters grow.

Four years into the future, the increase in motorised transport associated with the fishmeal factory has not led to the feared adaptation of motorcycles but a drastic increase in actual (car) taxis instead. The tension between motorised traffic and low-carbon mobility is contrary to 2015 participants' wish to avoid walking and cycling becoming 'overshadowed.' In 2019, the increased experience of motorised transport was a central discussion point for both women and male youth.

Women were predominately concerned with "careless driving" practices, including "dangerous overtaking," "overspeeding" and "unsafe parking" within Kartong, as well as "big lorries with poor br[ake]s" and "accidents" as a consequence of the above. As a case in point, during my visit to The Gambia in 2019, a new motorised tricycle less than a week old and handled by an unexperienced driver drove through a barbed wire fence when it came off a sandy road whilst carrying a group of children on the back. Unsurprisingly, by 2020, women wanted slow, careful and safe driving, seeing this as an urgent priority.

Male youth had similar concerns about "overspeeding," "careless," "unqualified" and "drunk drivers." Looking at a 2021–2025 timeframe, they want cars to move at low speed through Kartong and drivers to be "careful," "qualified" and "conscious." In addition, they did not want "roads without drainage" and listed specific equipment often missing in vehicles including "cars without seatbelts,' driving "without light or signal," "travel without fire extinguisher" or "first aid" kit. Instead they wanted "roads with drainage," "cars with seatbelts," "lights" and "signal," "fire extinguisher[s]" and "first aid" kits. Here it should be noted that about a third of male participants had driving licences. Compared with only one of the female participants being able to drive, this contributed to relatively greater awareness of what a car should be equipped with in the group of male youth.

Women expressed frustration about the quality of service including "no direct transport" connections and "increased fares at night," for example, for those returning from work at the fishmeal factory. This highlighted a gendered conflict related to transport practices and benefits where women passengers are at the mercy of fares set by male drivers. Women also complained of "overcrowded/overloaded" vehicles as well as "breakdowns" associated with "poorly maintained cars." By 2020, the women want to have access to "direct transport" connections, regulated taxi fares ("control fare") and passenger numbers ("up to maximum capacity," not more) as well as access to "well maintained vehicles."

Similarly, male youth complained about "cars with polluting engines" and the discomfort associated with "overloaded" vehicles. By 2025, they want cars in "good condition" and to replace bush taxis altogether with smaller taxis which will speed up journey times by reducing the need to stop along the way and drop off/pick up passengers which is similar to the notion of "small sizeable cars" that came up in 2013.

Also, women and male youth raised concerns about "carless" or "unsafe" cycling practices especially the use of "bikes without br[ake]s" and "without lights." In the near future they wanted safe cycling and well "maintained bikes with lights and br[ake]s." Related to this, male youth complained about "the same road for all users" and wanted "separate road[s] or paths "for different users" such as pedestrians, cyclists and cars. For women on the other hand a key concern was roaming livestock and "pig invasion." The wish for future "animal control" was tangentially related to stop roaming animals on the street but the discussion amongst women was more centred around the destructive nature animals have when they enter compounds at night as opposed to the obstruction they might pose for road users.

In 2019, river transport did not feature in the discussions of women and male youth who participated in the workshop. However, separately an oyster fisher who had been involved in the 2015 workshops stated her frustration over the increase in boats in parts of the Allahein river where oysters are grown, which is exactly what her group did not want to happen. She associated this with traffic to supply the fishmeal factory.[5]

Apart from increased numbers of boats on the river and a growing number of motorised vehicles traveling through Kartong, the fishmeal factory has also introduced a particular example of new transport technology in the community: an electric scooter used by factory staff. The scooter, which can regularly be seen traveling through the settlement area along the Kombo Coastal Road on its way to and from the factory, provides a visible technological alternative to conventional fossil-fuel based scooters and motorbikes.

However, the factory, which is not connected to the NAWEC grid, uses a diesel generator to generate electricity. As long as vehicles rely on power generated by off-grid diesel generators or by NAWEC, even electric vehicles (EVs) are part of a linear energy metabolism based on imported fossil fuels. In contrast, the village of Manduar, located just outside of Brikama, is home to 'Africa's first solar taxi.' The taxi is part of a research project and is charged by solar panels on the roof of a carport (Coker and Drammeh, 2018).

Replacing conventional vehicles with EVs used in the preceding examples could address the concern raised by male youth in Kartong and participants in 2013 about low quality second-hand motorised cars which currently make up a large proportion of vehicles operating in The Gambia (ADB, p. 15). However, new technology requires new technical skills training for maintenance and repair.

Nonetheless, with tangible examples available locally, it is not unthinkable that The Gambia may start to transition to electric vehicles in the not-too-distant future. However, it will only provide an opportunity to reduce fossil fuel dependence, if The Gambia is able to increase generating capacity of renewable electricity either on or off-grid.

Envisioning electricity access

The 2013 workshops coincided with the arrival of grid electricity in Kartong and access was therefore at the forefront of participant's minds, who did not want "a household, business, etc. in Kartong without access to power supply," "that cannot afford electricity" or suffers from "erratic power supply" caused by load shedding. "We do not want battery powered lamps" referring to small disposable batteries commonly used at that time, or "be without street lights all over Kartong." We don't [want] increase in power tariff" or "be energy vulnerable," for example, "not depend . . . on only national power grid."

Instead, by 2030 "we want constant power supply," "renewable energy" sources such as solar and wind, "we want electricity to be affordable to all the citizens of Kartong," and "we want all the street[s] to have light." "We want solar power . . . to be used in torch lights, radios, etc. " replacing disposable batteries and "we want to gain income from electricity e.g. by selling it to the main provider (e.g. NAWEC)." This is in the context of visiting the Batokunku wind turbine as part of the workshops (see Chapter 3).

In 2015, having gained more first-hand experience of grid electricity in the community, participants said "electricity should not be expensive," "unreliable" or "inaccessible." It should also "not cause harm," for example, cause fires or "pollute the environment." Instead, by 2030 "electricity should be affordable," "reliable" and "accessible to all" across the community. "It[s] consumption should be safe" and "it should be environmentally friendly." Furthermore, "electricity should generate employment."

Four years later, both women and male youth emphasised the need for uninterrupted as well as consistent power supply. Women did not "want power to [go] off" or for people to be excluded from applying for cash power metres "because of [limited] finances." Already by 2021 they envisioned "power to be on" and "easy access by areas not yet electrified." Similarly, male youth complained about "frequent power cuts" and the fact that grid access is "limited at one side of Kartong," despite everybody paying their taxes. They envisioned a future in 2025 with "stable power supply" and grid access "all over the village" because "everybody should be benefitting."

Women complained that "electricit[y] is very expensive because everyday you have to buy cash power," "if power goes off it [a]ffect[s] our business" and potential to generate income. Similarly, male youth were concerned about potential business losses especially where electricity is required to pay for rented spaces used for income generation activities such as a tailoring workshop. Women suggested that constant grid electricity would mean "business will continue."

Women also raised safety concerns and thought that using "switches" or "energy during thunder and lightning" could cause potential fires. Interestingly, they envisioned meters to be turned off to prevent damage rather than technological solutions to ensure safety. Distrust in technology is arguably exacerbated by examples such as that of a tailor who had applied for a cash power meter to run an electric sewing machine. The technician who came to install it missed off the circuit breaker switch, a vital component that protects the system from excess charge and subsequent equipment damage or fires. The tailor was unaware that there was anything missing until a local NAWEC employee noted the error and urged the tailor to report it. Locals had no doubt that the first technician had taken advantage of the unsuspecting tailor and sold the part on the black market.

Male youth were concerned about low quality wiring locally known as 'Dubai cables' and recalled examples where these had caused household fires. Instead they wanted "good wiring systems" used in buildings. They also complained about the fact that transmission lines, which carry higher voltage than the local distribution grid, run over people's houses. Previously, transmission cables had dropped on the ground in one of the participant's compound and people were afraid to walk past it. By 2025, the group envisions high tension lines to be put underground or alternatively for the point where the transmission changes to the local distribution grid would be taken out to the edge of the settlement area.

Finally, women suggested that "if power is always on and off it [a]ffected our properties," referring to the effects on appliances due to frequent blackouts. Constant supply would therefore ensure "there will be no breakdown." They also worried about "people . . . use[ing] broken socket[s]" which should be repaired "as soon as possible" and "receive[ing] calls while charging phones" which they associated with damage to the phones that can get very hot whilst plugged in. Male youth suggested frequent power cuts as well as fluctuations in voltage supplied by the grid contributed to the failure of fridges and televisions. Furthermore, some gadgets used in local households are second-hand imports from countries such as the US which have "different voltage systems" altogether, further increasing the problem. Finally, male youth were concerned that second-hand electronics were of poor quality and "some of them they consume more current than even you know it." In 2025, they want to have "new quality electric appliances" instead. At household level women also expressed concern about the lack of energy efficient gadgets and practices including high energy consuming appliances such as irons and kettles as well as "continuous use[] of bulb[s] in houses especially while sleeping." By 2021, they want these to be replaced with efficient alternatives and people to adapt their behaviour, for example, switching off lights at night.

Overall, women and male youth expressed more urgency reflected in much shorter timeframes than compared with the 2013 and 2015 workshop participants.

In addition, during the 2019 workshops, the issue of water scarcity was affecting people across the community and was exacerbated both by the lack of rainfall and intermittent grid electricity supply reducing the ability to pump water from the central borehole. It was therefore raised as a separate point during the visioning exercise.

For both women and male youth, having access to uninterrupted drinking water was a key priority. Both highlighted that a lack of electricity or cash power results in reduced water supply. "Here, if there is not electricity, there is no water or there is electricity [supply], the cash power has finished. We don't want that." Similarly, women do not want "cash power to get finish[ed] at a time that we are in need of water" and the water to "stop running."

By 2025 male youth want "constan[t] water supply" and "everybody to have access to water at their own vicinity." Similarly, by 2020–2021 women want "water to run always" and to have "enough water supply at home" instead of "carrying water from a very far distance." They initially saw having sufficient cash power as the solution but then discussed the long-term sustainability of this. One participant suggested that increasing the local generating capacity of solar energy was a better long-term solution, recognising the vulnerability of the community in a context of increasing fossil fuel dependence and not merely having sufficient energy to pump water but also "sustainable energy." Reflecting on one of the groups in the workshop she said:

> I was thinking there could be like a mechanism for . . . also have enough running water but in a way that is more sustainable . . . because . . . we were using solar. So instead of us buying cash power and using the cash power everyday . . . I was thinking that they were going to mention some sort of mechanisms of . . . going back to the solar system again or even bettering the situation with solar and some cash power.

In turn, this poses the question, what models could be adapted at community level to enable this?

A future with local renewable generating capacity

In 2005 the State House of The Gambia published the national Electricity Act under former President Yahya Jammeh, who at the time was also the Gambian Secretary of State for energy. A brief examination of the legislative document reveals that it enables private generators to connect to the NAWEC grid and as such was key in making the Batokunku development possible. Furthermore, the Renewable Energy Act 2013 offers the potential for distributed and locally owned renewable energy generation and requires the Public Utilities Regulatory Authority (PURA) to develop a Feed-In Tariff (FIT) (MoE, 2013). Over the lifetime of a renewable energy installation, FITs typically provide guaranteed payment tariffs to distributed power producers such as households when they feed renewable electricity into the national grid. As a policy mechanism, it thereby accelerates investments in renewable energy and has been widely adapted across the world including several African countries (Meyer-Renschhausen, 2013). It appears that the Gambian FIT is designed to provide a financial incentive for a 15-year period from the point of installation that benefits grid connected projects with a generating capacity of between 20 kW and 1.5 MW. This is much larger than a typical household installation and could therefore be suitable for sizeable community-based projects or public and industry buildings with large roof structures. Larger installations are envisioned to negotiate traditional Power Purchase Agreements whereas those under 20 kW "that are designed primarily to meet the customer's own demand" could be connected under Net Metering Agreements instead (UNIDO, 2013). The latter is therefore more suited to smaller households as well as community-based installations.

However, FITs have yet to become practically available and the connection rate of renewable energy across the country has been slow, adding to the overall pressure of providing ever-increasing electricity supply. Similarly, net metering is not practised widely in The Gambia. A notable exception is a 20 kW solar photovoltaic installation on the roof of Leo's Hotel in Brufut which is located north east of Batokunku (Figure 6.1).

A weak grid, which can only cope with a limited amount of intermittent renewables is a key stifling factor for connecting renewables in The Gambia (Diop et al., 2014, p. 26). Once the grid is strengthened the number of renewable energy schemes could drastically increase and thereby reduce the gap between energy demand and available access and supply.

In Kartong, the energy access gap could also be reduced through a Batokunku-like project. However, during a visit to Batokunku in 2013, Kartonkas met with members of the local VDC to learn about their experience, the benefits and challenges associated with the wind project. Subsequently, Kartonkas reflected on whether or not a mini-grid powered by renewables could be used to provide electricity to underserved parts of the Kartong settlement area in a similar set-up. While there are broader regulatory, technical and financing issues to be considered, there was a strong sense that in the specific socio-cultural context of Kartong, this would not be a viable

Figure 6.1 Kartonkas visit grid-connected solar installation at Leo's Hotel

option. It was felt that collecting electricity payments through a local committee and being responsible for a complex infrastructure project would lead to local tensions and should be the responsibility of entities such as NAWEC instead.

There are a number of other options available for Kartong to benefit from community-owned renewable energy which would provide additional generating capacity to meet the growing demand for electricity or provide income for the community as envisioned by workshop participants in 2013 (Box 6.1). In turn, this could be used for local development initiatives, raise funds towards the extension of grid infrastructure to the more recent settlement areas, or counter the increasing dependence on fossil fuels and associated costs.

Box 6.1   Potential options for community-owned renewable energy in Kartong

Option 1: the community owns grid-connected renewable energy generation

The community owns a local renewable energy generation asset such as a solar photovoltaic installation and is fully responsible for the development and day-to-day management of the project. This requires the community to develop strong regulatory and technical capabilities to take on the project related to raising and managing finance of the initial capital investment, design, ongoing maintenance costs and distribution of benefits. Alternatively, initial fundraising could be used to employ a development officer to lead the project development. A successful project could generate income for local development projects or subsidise costs associated with buying in other energy services such as grid electricity.

Governance and finance

The VDC may wish to set up a subsidiary to develop the project. The main purpose of this would be to generate income for local development initiatives, which may initially be focused on energy related projects such as grid extensions to underserved areas. There should also be a contractual agreement that adequately compensates the landowner for the duration of the project. Furthermore, it would be advisable to enter an agreement with a company for ongoing technical maintenance, similar to the Batokunku project which employs an engineering firm in neighbouring Tujereng.

Finance could be raised through donations, selling co-operative shares, loans or a combination thereof. Contributors may include Kartong diaspora, donations from donor agencies or money (donations or investments) raised through an online crowdfunding platform. The project may also benefit from the Gambian Renewable Energy Fund or FIT as required to be set up by PURA under the Renewable Energy Act 2013 (Singh et al., 2013).

Option 2: the community shares ownership of local renewable energy generation

In a 'shared ownership' project the community collaborates with a renewable energy developer such as a commercial partner or a non-governmental organisation with relevant expertise. Together the partnership develops a solar photovoltaic (or other renewable energy) installation that feeds electricity into the grid for which it receives payments in return. The community benefits from working with a strong partner that has expertise in developing renewable energy projects, understands the legal context of The Gambia and financing models and can mitigate potential risks. So-called 'virtual' ownership means the community owns a share in the overall development which in physical terms may equate to a number of solar panels but is really a share in the profit generation based on the financial contribution by the community and subsequent share in costs and benefits. If the aim is to raise finance for local development initiatives there is no additional benefit in owning the actual asset. While the potential income generated will be less compared with a wholly community-owned project, the project risks and management burdens are also significantly reduced in a shared ownership project.

The commercial partner benefits by having the support of the local community who make land available to develop the scheme, have an intrinsic interest to look after the installation and may otherwise object on the grounds of local resources being exploited by external agencies with no direct benefit to the local community (see sand mining).

Governance and finance

Similar to Batokunku, the Kartong VDC could establish an energy committee. However, instead of taking responsibility for the day-to-day operations of the installed system the committee would be responsible for raising funds for its (virtual) stake in the first instance and manage subsequent income through a Community Benefit Fund (CBF). The committee's main purpose would be to allocate profits generated for the CBF to fund local development initiatives that benefit the wider community. Transparent processes used to govern the committee and identify initiatives to be funded will help mitigate tensions in the community. Annual grant allocation rounds could also minimise the burden of financial management of the CBF. The overall share in the project will depend on how much money the community is able to raise in relation to the overall cost of the project. However, this would likely be restricted to a maximum of 49% if a commercial partner is taking on the majority of the development burden, risk and day-to-day management of the installation.

Furthermore, there should be a contractual agreement that adequately compensates the landowner for the duration of the project.

Similar to Option 1, the community's financial share in the development could be raised through donations, co-operative shares, loans or a combination thereof. Again, contributors may include Kartong diaspora, charitable donations or money (donations or investments) raised through an online crowdfunding platform. The project may also benefit from the Gambian Renewable Energy Fund or FITs to be set up by PURA.

There is also the possibility for Kartong to approach renewables by thinking about particular energy services to the community, for example in relation to communication or water supply. Communication infrastructure such as mobile phone receptor masts have in the past used an array of different forms of electricity generation for the required power, including solar energy. However, as these are owned and operated by national service providers, there is little possibility for the community to influence or manage installations. In contrast, water supply infrastructure is owned by the community and there are several options to reduce the ongoing cost associated with buying in grid electricity to power pumps and provide more reliable supply.

Firstly, the community already owns a small solar photovoltaic installation which previously provided power to pump water into the central water storage tank. If connected to the grid it could generate a small amount of income to subsidise costs associated with purchasing electricity from NAWEC to supply water. However, even if a FIT was available, this current installation is too small to meet the 20 kW threshold.

Secondly, discussions with members of the Kartong water committee suggest that there is potential to connect the existing solar panels to another borehole nearby which has not been used due to salt intrusion but could provide additional capacity if it went deeper into the water table. If a feasibility study shows this is a viable option it could reduce the burden to pay for NAWEC electricity unless the additional borehole is only used as backup during periods of load shedding.

Thirdly, as one of the female workshop participants suggested, the capacity of the solar panels could be increased to be able to power the new pump and so reduce dependence on expensive and fossil-fuel–based grid electricity by providing a more sustainable alternative. The connection to NAWEC could be used as a backup and to compensate for reduced solar generation during nighttime and depending on weather conditions. This would make the water supply system more resilient whilst reducing overall running costs. Here, net metering, similar to the roof-top installation at Leo's hotel, would also enable excess generating capacity to be fed into the grid and generate income in the form of the meter running backwards. While national generating capacity is unable to supply sufficient electricity, an agreement with NAWEC to concentrate load shedding in Kartong during daylight hours when solar photovoltaic cells are most productive would also reduce gaps in water supply.

Arguably, any of the options are better than keeping an expensive asset lying obsolete in the form of unused solar panels. The community needs to weigh up what will provide the most reliable and cost-effective water supply long-term. As one of the male participants in 2019 put it: "We want sufficient water supply, we don't want this on and off, when there is electricity we have when there is not we don't have."

Once metering is introduced, water consumption in Kartong is likely to take an initial dip before increasing in line with a growing population and installations of private household taps within compounds and individual households. Therefore, building in the ability to grow with changing consumption levels through modular approaches, for example, is key. As demonstrated in previous chapters, infrastructure that is implemented for the now does not simply remain fit for the future; it needs to adapt.

Capacity building to enable adaptation of sustainable practices

Since the first visioning workshops a significant period of time has passed during which access to modern energy has been distributed unequally and Kartong has continued to follow a conventional development trajectory to become increasingly dependent on imported fossil fuels. While this suggests that the community is being locked into a linear energy metabolism in the long-term, there are opportunities to shift towards more sustainable and equitable mechanisms to provide modern energy as well as respond to wider development challenges in Kartong.

Back in 2015 participants wished for electricity to generate employment opportunities, which it arguably has. From electric fridges which are used to chill drinks, or the 'car wash' which relies on an electric hoover, new and informal sectors have sprung up locally. Furthermore, installing grid-connected renewable energy could generate finance for local development projects as outlined earlier. However, thus far, Kartong has struggled to adequately maintain community energy projects and there are also maintenance challenges at household level in relation to energy generation (e.g. off-grid solar) and energy-consuming appliances.

While financing is a challenge, Kartong has been able to tap into foreign donors, local Gambian and diaspora networks to raise substantial funds for projects at community level (e.g. the upgrade of central water supply; grid extensions), but has struggled with successfully negotiating socio-cultural structures to raise money and maintain projects locally. Here, capacity building aimed at enabling local governance of projects can help navigate complex socio-cultural structures in which payment collection in particular can place a huge burden on individuals. This could be capacity building at local governance or project level.

It is suggested that "communities can ensure the sustainability of projects, but require support from a wider repair and maintenance supply chain that is easily accessible" (Practical Action, 2018, p. 7). In Kartong, maintenance supply chains of course enable (fixing bicycles) or hinder (broken computer) repairs. This deserves further attention, especially as new electric gadgets and equipment such as scooters, televisions and fridges become available. Furthermore, the use of 'low-efficiency' second-hand equipment and appliances is an issue raised in several of the workshops that can also be observed in other parts of West Africa (e.g. Gyamfi et al., 2018). Whilst regulation of second-hand goods (e.g. to provide energy ratings) may improve appliances available, capacity building to improve energy literacy at a local level could also enable consumers to make better purchasing decisions. In terms of households, this should be targeted especially at women, who are traditionally responsible for domestic spheres which is unlikely to change drastically in the near future. Local insight based on gendered practices also emerged in the 2019 workshops: in relation to cooking, women offered rocket stove technology as a potential solution, whereas male youth voiced more ambiguous visions about non-polluting equipment. In contrast, when discussing transport, male youth who were more likely to have obtained driving licences, also provided more specific ideas of the type of equipment a car should have to be deemed safe.

To enable long-term access to sufficient energy, capacity building would benefit from a more holistic approach that includes supporting governance structures to maintain and repair community-owned infrastructure, enabling smart purchasing decisions at household level as well as building technical capabilities to carry out repairs.

Notes

1 This was based on an exercise during the 2012 Global Solutions Lab led by Medard Gabel from BigPictureSmallWorld, Inc. and hosted at Chestnut College in Philadelphia.
2 Personal conversation, Kartong, July 2019.
3 It should be noted that local industries including fish smoking facilities on the river and beach sides as well as several bakeries did not feature in the discussions.
4 The term is derived from the name of the Indonesian capital.
5 Personal conversation, Kartong, July 2019.

References

ADB (2016) *The Gambia: Transport sector diagnostic study*. Abidjan: African Development Bank.

Coker, O. and Drammeh, R. (2018) Africa's first solar taxi launched in Gambia. *The Standard* [Online], 5 July. Available from: <https://standard.gm/africas-first-solar-taxi-launched-in-gambia/> [Accessed 12 August 2019].

Diop, D., Zwanenburg, M. and Pasdeloup, M.V. (2014) *The Gambia SE4ALL: Action agenda*. Brussels: BizClim.

Gyamfi, S., Diawuo, F.A., Kumi, E.N., Sika, F. and Modjinou, M. (2018) The energy efficiency situation in Ghana. *Renewable and Sustainable Energy Reviews*, 82 (1), pp. 1415–1423. https://doi.org/10.1016/j.rser.2017.05.007

KART (2005) *Kartong's responsible tourism policy*. Kartong: Kartong Association for Responsible Tourism.

Meyer-Renschhausen, M. (2013) Evaluation of feed-in tariff-schemes in African countries. *Journal of Energy in Southern Africa*, 24 (1), pp. 56–66. https://doi.org/10.17159/2413-3051/2013/v24i1a3008

MoE (2013) *Renewable Energy Act 2013*. Banjul: Ministry of Energy.

Practical Action (2018) *Poor people's energy outlook 2018: Achieving inclusive energy access at scale*. Rugby: Practical Action Publishing. https://doi.org/10.3362/9781780447544

SEforALL (2012) *Sustainable energy for all rapid assessment and gap analysis: The Gambia*. Vienna/ Washington: United Nations Development Programme and Sustainable Energy for All.

Singh, G., Nouhou, S.A. and Sokona, M.Y. (2013) *The Gambia: Renewables readiness assessment 2013*. Abu Dhabi: International Renewable Energy Agency.

Sovacool, B.K. (2012) The political economy of energy poverty: A review of key challenges. *Energy for Sustainable Development*, 16 (3), pp. 272–282. https://doi.org/10.1016/j.esd.2012.05.006

UNIDO (2013) *Feed-in tariff model and standard PPA*. Vienna: United Nations Industrial Development Organization.

7 Reframing energy access
A chance for fair and sustainable consumption

Situated insight in the context of energy access dynamics

A decade of regular immersions in the Gambian community of Kartong, accompanied by explorations of historic changes and potential energy futures, have led to deeper and situated insight into people's practices and the factors that shape them. The local energy metabolism is evidently the result of the culmination of intersecting socio-cultural, socio-economic, socio-environmental, socio-political as well as socio-technical dynamics.

Socio-cultural factors include largely distinct gender roles that are reflected in different energy practices between men and women, where female energy consumption continues to revolve more around domestic spheres. This includes socio-economic activities that use technologies available at home and informal businesses based on food and drink provision. In contrast to women, men have been more likely to adapt transport-related technologies including bicycles and cars (though recently there has also been an increase in female cyclists and motorists). Again, this has been associated with gendered employment opportunities.

Long-established sharing practices across extended family and friendship networks account for another important socio-cultural dimension. Historically, sharing practices ensured families were fed across the community whilst today sharing also helps negotiate access to electricity for many energy-scarce households in Kartong. Similarly, economic benefits are likely shared within existing social networks. Arguably, this makes the community as a whole more resilient. However, it also places an economic burden on individuals who may feel social pressure to support others, thereby reducing the capabilities to establish and maintain community-owned infrastructure, especially where this requires fee collection.

Everyday including socio-economic energy practices continue to follow annual cycles of dry and rainy seasons. The former is associated with economic opportunities related to tourism and vegetable growing. Domestically, locals are likely to heat water for showers during this time, especially at night or when the cool Harmattan winds blow from the Sahara Desert. During the hot and humid rainy season, electric fans are used instead to keep indoor temperatures down.

Available technology and infrastructure developments have been greatly influenced by political events and successive governments. Economic insecurity around political unrest in the 1990s indirectly led to the first local electricity grid which for a short while powered street lights in Kartong. Wider political changes at the time are associated with subsequent improvements in communication services and road construction which connects Kartong to other parts in The Gambia. More recently, rural electrification has enabled widespread adaptation of electricity and electrical equipment across households connected to the grid, changing domestic practices and providing new economic opportunities.

However, access to infrastructure, energy services and associated economic benefits have not been delivered equitably across the community. Socially differentiated practices, especially regarding gender have been more likely to exclude or disadvantage women. Furthermore, spatial inequality regarding energy access is often discussed in terms of the rural-urban divide. However, the research clearly shows that there are also stark differences between neighbouring and within communities. The immigrant settlement of Madina Salam has been excluded from rural electrification altogether unlike its three neighbours of Kartong, Berending and Gunjur. In Kartong, more recently established parts of the village are still not covered by grid infrastructure therefore enduring energy scarcity. In contrast, those that are connected are likely on a path to future overconsumption instead of energy sufficiency.

In the process of gaining increasing access to modern energy services, Kartong has moved from a predominately circular energy metabolism based on local resources such as wood fuel to ever-growing dependence on imported fossil fuels. This includes a shift towards fossil-fuel–based transport, grid electricity used for domestic and business purposes as well as to provide energy for pumping water from the central borehole. Kartong has neither leapfrogged to modern energy based on renewables, nor have energy services ensured sufficient access for all.

A more holistic understanding of energy access dynamics is needed to adequately assess metabolic processes of energy systems. However, this has to go beyond relating different types of infrastructure such as electricity and transport to one another. Rather, it requires integrating policy with situated insight that connects the technical with the non-technical aspects of energy in everyday life, specifically people's practices, socio-cultural values and aspirations.

Concluding remarks

As the reader you will hopefully have gathered that this book has not been about arguing against technological or infrastructural developments. It does however advocate for a shift in focus where situated insight is recognised as integral to designing equitable and sustainable energy futures instead of a tokenistic consultation tick box after the fact. Dominant techno-centric, albeit well-intended, approaches have failed to consider wider intersecting dynamics which have and continue to shape energy scarcity and energy access at local level. Importantly, these dynamics do not just add complexity that may lead to failed interventions if overlooked or marginalise parts of society if ignored. Instead, I suggest a more optimistic view in that these also offer opportunities for social innovations. What if deeply rooted values of sharing practices observed in Kartong could be built upon to develop formalised structures that help deliver more equitable energy access across the community without placing pressures on individuals? What if instead of marginalising women, deeper insight into their lived experience is used to create targeted capacity building to strengthen their voice in energy governance that in turn leads to increased benefits for local families as a whole. What if changes into energy practices are better understood to design more flexible and resilient infrastructure projects that are able to adapt to the needs of changing demographics or encourage more sufficient and thereby sustainable consumption levels in the long run? Ultimately reframing energy access by looking at it through a more situated lens will enable us to work with instead of against people.

I will leave you to contemplate a number of recommendations and considerations regarding energy access with relevance for policy makers and practitioners.

Key recommendations to re-frame energy access

Consider gendered energy practices

In the Gambian context examined here, energy practices remain highly gendered with women responsible for domestic spheres and often engaged in entrepreneurial activities related to food. Instead of making generalised claims, the benefits of access to modern energy therefore need to be understood along these gendered lines. For example, it can broadly be argued that access to electricity coupled with mobile phone technology has significantly improved access to modern communication for the community. However, a more gendered perspective highlights that women of a certain age are less likely to share in the benefits of this as they are less likely to be literate and therefore less able to use common functions such as texting or searching the web (Munro and Schiffer, 2019).

It is important to understand that a techno-centric approach to development, where the urgency to enable access to other modern energy services such as electricity might inadvertently further exacerbate gender gaps, if it fails to consider gendered practices. Insight into the differences of energy practices between men and women can ensure more equitable distribution of benefits by developing targeted interventions.

> *What if women were better equipped to choose energy efficient appliances when they make domestic purchasing decisions? What if investment in communication infrastructure was integrated with programmes to improve adult literacy skills? What if capacity building of women ensured that their needs were better represented in energy governance, shaping policies and infrastructure programmes which also affect their lives?*

Ensure rural electrification covers entire settlement areas

Partial electrification exacerbates existing and creates new spatial inequalities both within and between settlements. The gap actually continues to widen as those with access continue to adapt new technologies or energy services for domestic and business purposes. Furthermore, those left behind are likely to be already experiencing other forms of resource scarcity. Finally, partial electrification undermines any community-wide efforts to develop energy access as electrified parts of the settlement no longer see this as an urgent priority.

> *What are the socio-economic benefits if an entire settlement is electrified at the same time (or electrification starts with the outskirts and less established parts)? What if instead of further marginalising immigrant communities and recent settlements, these share in the benefits of electrification programmes?*

Build sufficiency into energy access projects and programmes to encourage sustainable consumption behaviour

To achieve sustainable levels of energy consumption, access to modern energy needs to go beyond basic levels of access and 'limited opportunity models' which only work for people as long as they are poor (Bhushan and Kumar, 2012). However, in the urgency to deliver first-time access, future overconsumption or 'energy addiction' is often not considered, despite being key to achieving sustainable consumption levels and development longer-term.[1] Sufficient energy requires both practical design considerations to embed sufficient consumption behaviour, as well as policy instruments.

> *What if rural electrification programmes used situated insight to enable sufficient consumption levels from the onset? What if in the context of finite generating capacity, consumption limits were carefully negotiated to enable more equitable supply to more households?*

Develop integrated approaches that go beyond technology

In Kartong, the culmination of different energy services at household and community level demonstrates a wider move towards increased fossil fuel dependence. Hence, a more holistic understanding of the energy metabolism including the resource flows of a range of different energy services such as transport, household electricity or energy to pump water is useful to assess wider trends. However, a more integrated approach also requires a move beyond the technical dimensions of energy consumption to include human insight and the factors that shape everyday practices.

> *What if the relationship between women's income generation activities and access to transport was better understood? Could it be used to negotiate consistent transport tariffs to provide more reliable income for women working in the local fishing industry? What if household gadgets were actually designed to be shared amongst extended family compounds? Could they be developed to be more robust to accommodate for different styles and higher volumes of usage?*

Don't 'just' donate infrastructure

It is relatively easy for charitable organisations to raise funds for visibly tangible energy infrastructure projects related to education, water access or healthcare. In Kartong new solar panels to provide water access through the central borehole came from one such donation, initially benefitting people across the settlement area. However, infrastructure can quickly become obsolete if it is not maintained or as in this case fails to account for future growth. In Kartong, the solar system could not meet growing demand for electricity to pump water which in turn was needed to cope with increasing levels of water consumption. As a result, expensive infrastructure is collecting dust and well-intended financial donations lie wasted.

> *What if infrastructure and donor grants were designed to be modular, enabling future growth? What if infrastructure was not donated but*

leased for the period of time it provides benefits and ready to be re-deployed elsewhere or re-manufactured after that?

Develop regional capacity building for alternative finance and ownership models of renewable energy

In The Gambia, limited technical skills available within the country to design, install and maintain renewable energy infrastructures are currently being addressed through the recent creation of a targeted energy curriculum. However, renewable energy can also be developed through a range of alternative ownership and financing models. This will enable communities to participate and share in the benefits of energy generation beyond simply consuming power whilst also contributing to reduced dependence on imported fossil fuels.

There are opportunities to learn from the huge variety of community energy projects in the European context (e.g. Roberts, 2014; Schiffer, 2014, 2017). However, the socio-economic, -political, -cultural, -environmental and -technical contexts of the Gambia and other ECOWAS and sub-Saharan countries would benefit from a regional capacity-building network that explores the potential of context-specific ownership and financing models and their relation to national and regional energy policy.

What if an online platform to fund energy access projects could be utilised to increase the impact of remittance payments already made to local communities? What if community ownership models were developed to build on existing legal and governance structures? What if mentoring schemes enabled peer-to-peer learning between different communities with varying levels of energy access? What if local energy projects could be used to increase national generating capacity whilst creating income streams to fund local development initiatives?

Consider seasonal changes

In The Gambia, there are distinct differences in energy practices between the dry and the rainy season. In addition, practices during Ramadan differ greatly from the rest of the year suggesting both socio-environmental and socio-cultural seasons of practice. Any technical interventions such as improved cooking stoves need to be rooted in insight of these seasonal differences.

Similarly, the wider socio-economic impact of 'seasonality' on energy access such as the ability to raise funds for grid connections at household level also needs to be understood and considered (Chambers, p. 69).

What if first-time grid access that requires households to make sub-stantial financial contributions in the form of connection fees is carefully timed to become available when seasonal income is at its highest? What are the implications for 'clean cooking' projects if they consider seasonal changes in cooking practices and available energy sources? What are the seasonal implications for achieving sufficient levels of energy consumption?

Note

1 The term energy addiction used here is inspired by a recent comment made by Alessandro Blasi (2019) at the IEA on the agency's 2019 edition of the World Energy Outlook: "what emerge is that more than #energytransition we are heading towards #energyaddiction."

References

Bhushan, C. and Kumar, J. (2012) *Going remote: Re-inventing the off-grid solar revolution for clean energy for all*. New Delhi: Centre for Science and Environment.

Blasi, A. (2019) *LinkedIN post: The new IEA's World Energy Outlook is out!* [Online]. November. Available from: <www.linkedin.com/in/alessandro-blasi-6579a66/detail/recent-activity/shares/> [Accessed 9 November 2019].

Chambers, R. (2012) *Provocations for development*. Warwickshire: Practical Action.

Munro, P.G. and Schiffer, A. (2019) Ethnographies of electricity scarcity: Mobile phone charging spaces and the recrafting of energy poverty in Africa. *Energy and Buildings*, 188–189, pp. 175–183. https://doi.org/10.1016/j.enbuild.2019.01.038

Roberts, J., Bodman, F. and Rybski, R. (2014) *Community power: Model legal frameworks for citizen-owned renewable energy*. London: ClientEarth.

Schiffer, A. (2017) *Shared ownership in Scotland: Opening up citizen participation in renewable energy*. Edinburgh: Friends of the Earth Scotland.

Schiffer, A. (2016) Empowered, excited, or disenfranchised? Unveiling issues of energy access inequality and resource dependency in the Gambia. *Energy Research & Social Science*, 18 August, pp. 50–61.

Schiffer, A. (2014) *Community power Scotland: From remote island grids to urban solar cooperatives*. Edinburgh: Friends of the Earth Scotland.

Glossary of local language terms and phrases

Alkalo   Traditional leader of the community

Ataya   Bittersweet tea, commonly brewed across The Gambia

Back way   Describes refugee route to Europe

Bah   Big or large, often used in conjunction with names or other nouns (see *Jabang Kunda-bah, Bum-bah* or *Pitipiti-bah*)

Balanta   Ethnic group that originates in Guinea Bissau

Bonga   Type of fish, commonly smoked to preserve it

Bum-bah   Large bedroom shared by women and children

Bush taxi   Minivan used as taxi for larger numbers of passengers

Compound   Extended family home consisting of several households (*see kunda*)

Coose   Type of grain (Digitaria exelis)

Dalasi   Gambian currency

Diaro   Name of early settler family in Kartong

Dubai cables   Electric cables and wires perceived to be of low quality

Faro   Rice field

Findo   Millet, a type of cereal crop

Folonko   Name of sacred crocodile pool in Kartong

Harmattan   Dusty seasonal wind blowing from the Sahara Desert

Jabang   Family name

Jabang Kunda-bah   Compound of the first Jabang family which settled in Kartong

Jabang Kunda-ring   Compound of the Jabang family which settled in Kartong after *Jabang Kunda-bah*

Jakarta   Adapted from the Indonesian capital to refer to motorcycle taxis

Jola   Ethnic group

Kabilo   Clan area; ward

Kafo   Social group based on age, sex and/or common interest

Karoninka   Ethnic group related to the Jola, found in southern Gambia and the Casamance region of southern Senegal

Kartonka   A person from Kartong

Koriteh   Muslim celebration that marks the end of Ramadan

Kunda   Extended family home consisting of several households (see *compound*); used in conjunction with the surname of a family that lives or has settled there

Mandinka   The Gambia's largest ethnic group and dominant language; most commonly spoken language in Kartong

Manneh   Family name

Na domo   Come eat

Njebe   Spicy bean dish

Pamparan   Fencing material derived from the top of palm trees

Pitipiti-bah   Local name given to noisy motorcycle once found in Kartong. The first part is an onomatopoeia mimicking the sound, the second meaning big (see *bah*).

Ring   Small; often used in conjunction with names and other nouns

Senfu   Type of bread

Sonko   Name of early settler family in Kartong

Tabula   A type of drum

Tambakulo   Popular round fruit with a large stone traditionally used as alternative to charcoal

Tapalapa   Baguette-like bread

Toubab   White person

Tourey   Family name

Video club   Local form of cinema popular for showing football matches

Wolof   Ethnic group and language spoken in The Gambia and most common local language in Senegal

Wonjo   Drink prepared from hibiscus leaves

Appendix 1
Energy Futures Workshop

The following text has been adapted from a capacity building handout prepared for Kartong participants in the 2019 Energy Futures Workshops funded through the BA/Leverhulme Small Grants scheme. It provides an overview of methods and underlying design-thinking framework used. The latter is derived from the UK Design Council's 'double diamond' process* while facilitation methods have been adapted from the 2012 Design Science Lab in Philadelphia, Friends of the Earth and other activist workshops I have attended over the years.

What is design thinking?

While the term design is often used to describe a particular outcome such as a product or building, here we are concerned with the design process as a methodology for solving problems or innovating. When this process is applied outside traditional disciplines (e.g. architecture or product design) it is referred to as 'design thinking.'** Importantly, the design-thinking process should be human-centred, which means it should reflect on the experiences, knowledge and aspirations of a particular group of people. It can be divided into a series of two repeating phases, referred to as 'divergent' and 'convergent' thinking (Figure A1).

Divergent thinking is all about generating new possibilities. Convergent thinking is concerned with making decisions, for example identifying priorities (Figure A2). The following exercises can be used to inform these phases.

Spectrum lines (divergent thinking)

Ask people to stand up in a space that is big enough for them to move from left to right. When you make a statement, such as 'my house has grid electricity' or 'I frequently travel outside of Kartong,' ask participants to think

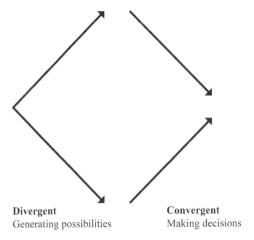

Figure A1   Divergent/convergent thinking phases

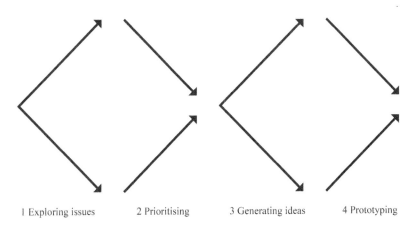

Figure A2   Underlying design-thinking process

about their personal experience. If the statement applies to them, ask them to move to the left side of the space, if it doesn't, ask them to the right and if it applies to some extent, they should move to the middle accordingly. Ask participants on different parts of the spectrum specific follow-up questions about their experience. For example, 'you say you frequently travel outside of Kartong, where do you travel to and why?'

This is a useful energiser or warm-up exercise that helps the facilitator and participants alike to find out information about other participants' experiences, including differences and commonalities. It can also be used to manage expectations about the workshop. Try and start with a simple generic statement such as 'I was born in this town' to make sure everyone understands the exercise before you move on. All you need to do is prepare a short list of ten or so statements.

Envisioning positive futures (divergent thinking)

Paradoxically it makes sense not to start with asking people to imagine ideal future scenarios. This can be daunting for some and will likely result in vague statements about sustainable living. In contrast, many people find it easier to think about their everyday experiences and complain about what is wrong with the local transport system, their child's school or the local water supply. Therefore, it is crucial not to tell people that they are embarking on a visioning exercise. Instead ask participants to 'complain,' but do so in a structured way by focusing on a specific issue in a particular context:

I/we don't want transport [issue] in Kartong [context] to . . .

- be expensive
- be overcrowded
- use poorly maintained vehicles
- be dependent on fossil fuels
- use unqualified drivers
- pose a danger because of speeding
- . . . . . .

Use a piece of paper that everyone can see and appoint a note taker to list complaints that participants are shouting out. Once this negative list is exhausted, and only then, ask people to turn these into opposites or positive alternatives. Change 'I/we don't want . . . ' to 'I/we want . . . .' Make sure the person who is writing is using a different coloured pen (indicated here by strikethrough and italic text):

I/we ~~don't~~ want transport in Kartong to . . .

- be ~~expensive~~ *affordable*
- be ~~overcrowded~~ *comfortable*
- use *well* ~~poorly~~ maintained vehicles
- ~~be dependent on fossil fuels~~ *use renewable/ clean fuel*

- use ~~un~~qualified drivers
- ~~pose a danger because of speeding~~ *drive at a safe speed*
- . . . . . .

If you have previously divided people into different groups, make sure each group presents their negatives/positives to the rest of the participants so that these can add missing points, ask for clarifications or offer different perspectives.

Finally, get the group to think about when they wish to see these positive changes and commit to a date. Now you have your vision for the future:

> *In 2025* I/we want transport in Kartong to *be affordable, comfortable, use well maintained vehicles, use renewable/ clean fuel, ...*

Tips: When participants choose a date remember that 'by tomorrow' is too short to be realistic, while the year 2100 is likely too far in the future to stimulate necessary action; use two different colours for positives and negatives to make the differences visible; get people to shout out negatives/positives and note them down on a large piece of paper that everyone can see or divide people into smaller groups.

Prioritising with dots (convergent thinking)

Now it is time to prioritise the points on your positive list(s). If participant groups have generated different lists for areas such as transport and electricity, make sure everyone has time to look at all of the sheets laid out. Pair illiterate participants with someone who can read. Ask people to draw dots next to the issues they see as most important. You can ask people to add one dot per sheet OR three dots across several sheets (including three next to the same point raised if they feel strongly about one particular issue). When everyone has added their dots, the points on your list with most dots are your priorities moving forward. However, these are not set in stone, especially if the views of minority groups are underrepresented. For example, what if only one of a group of ten people lacks access to grid electricity and the others therefore do not see gaining access as a priority?

Frame your priority as a question (convergent thinking)

In order to kick-start the next phase of divergent thinking, try and frame your priorities as questions, which makes it easier to generate ideas. Use this formula which asks you to consider who your target is and what you want them to do:

'How can we get [actor] to [action]?'

Example:

'How can we get [taxi drivers] in Kartong to [drive slowly]'?
How can we [get NAWEC] to [provide electricity access to all households in Kartong]?'

Tip: This is harder than it looks. If both your actor and your action are too broad, try adding a specific context such as [in Kartong]. If you have several priorities you want to work on, generate a question for each instead of one question that tries to encompass all.

Generate possibilities through brainstorming (divergent thinking)

Brainstorming is a technique that can be used to generate ideas as part of the 'divergent' phase in the design process. Participants collectively come up with ideas in response to the questions generated in the previous exercise. These should provide enough focus to brainstorm around a specific issue but be open enough to generate a range of different possibilities. During brainstorming, participants should follow these rules:

*   Don't judge ideas ('but that won't work . . .')
*   Encourage wild ideas
*   Build on the ideas of others

One person can write down ideas while participants are discussing the issue. If there are some people in the group who dominate the conversation through lengthy monologues whilst others tend to be quiet, try using sticky notes. Participants are only allowed to draw/write one idea per sticky note. Using sticky notes means you can also group ideas later on.

Asset mapping*** (divergent thinking)

Now that you have your priorities, it is time to start thinking about how you can get there. Mapping your community's 'assets' is a good place to start. If you can, write/draw on/with different coloured sticky notes and marker pens. Alternatively, just use different coloured pens (three distinct colours). Get your group of people (5–30) to stand around one large piece of paper or clean surface so that everyone can see and participate. If some people in your group are illiterate, make sure they are partnered with someone who can read and write. Focus on a particular issue such as developing a renewable energy project, a community garden or providing sustainable access to clean water. Ask people to write assets on sticky notes (one per sticky note) and stick them onto the paper. Break your assets down into several categories such as a) individuals/people with relevant knowledge, skills and experience; b) institutions/ organisations in or outside of the community, and c) specific places that relate positively to your issue.

Make sure that your assets are specific, e.g. avoid 'someone who works at NAWEC' and say 'Fatou Ceesay, technician at NAWEC' instead. Reassure people that they can write down the same asset as someone else and that there will likely be overlap between different types of assets such as particular institutions/organisations and individuals that work there. Finish one asset category using one colour before you move to the next category and switch colour. When all assets are laid out, get people to look at the huge map of assets they can build upon. Now you need to start to group assets into themes, e.g. ones that relate to a specific issue such as water access, governance, fundraising, etc. If you have not used sticky notes, you can write on a separate piece of paper to do this. If one asset comes up over and over again, this could indicate that it is a particularly valuable asset.

Tip: An asset does not have to be someone with specific technical expertise, but could also be an individual who is good at mobilising people.

Prototyping your ideas (convergent thinking)

To test and refine your ideas (convergent thinking) 'prototype' them. This can include drawing, physical mock-ups and acting out scenarios. The idea is to fail 'often and early' or to 'fail forward' by spending relatively little resource (e.g. money) trying something out before committing to a specific project. For example, if you are designing a community garden, use sticks and rope in a field to test your layout and act out scenarios of how people might use the space.

* www.designcouncil.org.uk/
** Brown, T. (2009) Change by Design: how design thinking transforms organizations and inspires innovation. New York: Harper Business.
*** Kretzmann, J. and McKnight, J. (1993) Building Communities From the Inside Out: a path toward finding and mobilizing a community's assets. Chicago: ACTA Publications.

Index

Page numbers in *italics* indicate Figures.

Printed in the United States
by Baker & Taylor Publisher Services